Nar Survivor

2 Books in 1

Elena Miro

<u>Disclaimer notice:</u>

Table of Contents

My Toxic Husband

Loving and Breaking Up with a Narcissistic Man—Start Your Psychopath-free Life Now!

Elena Miro

This book is based on a true story involving real people. Certain names and identifying information have been adjusted to protect their privacy.

From Author

Dear Reader,

After having personally suffered from narcissistic abuse, writing this book was a passionate and healing project for me. In addition, part of that passion is helping others who may be suffering from the same trauma.

I thought of you feeling like you're going crazy, suffering from the shaming and guilt trips your toxic partner puts you through, and feeling trapped in a loveless, emotionally abusive relationship as I wrote these books.

I wrote *My Toxic Husband* and a *FREE YOURSELF* (trauma and recovery workbook for women) to help you find the answers you're seeking and the clarity you deserve.

If you're reading these books, I'm sure it's because you're suffering in an emotionally abusive relationship, or you may have just gotten out of one and are feeling lost and confused. You might be thinking you're to blame for what happened, and it's quite likely your loved one told you just that, whether directly or in more subtle, manipulative ways.

You might feel as though you've lost contact with reality, you might doubt yourself and what you thought you knew to be true, and you might even have suffered physical ailments as a result of the abuse you endured. You might also feel as though your inner light is less bright as a result. However, that light still shines, and part of my desire is to help you bring it back to that glowing brilliance that brightens everyone around you.

To do that, you first have to face some confusing and painful memories with bravery. It's probably true that your narcissistic abuser was well-liked, perhaps even revered in their profession or admired as a guru or therapist. To others who aren't as close as an intimate partner, they will likely appear successful, sincere, and charming. However, you know the truth.

I know what it is like to feel what you're going through now. I was deeply in love with my narcissistic abuser, and I felt the pain of the sudden personality shift that happened as he revealed his true nature to me. I felt my life, energy, self-esteem, and self-confidence all draining away, leaving only an exhausted husk of a person behind.

Pathological narcissism is a confusing, crazy, and disturbing mental condition to deal with, and if you've been in an intimate relationship with someone who suffers from this, you've been the recipient of the full force of their abusive behavior.

I escaped my abuser, but the experience left me confused, angry, and traumatized. As part of my recovery process, I began to learn everything I could about this insidious condition. I even earned a degree in psychology so I could understand all the others. I also decided to write a book about my experience, so I could help other people who are going through the same thing. In fact, I decided to write two books: one on my experiences in a toxic relationship, and then a workbook to help with the recovery process.

In preparation for these books, I did extensive research into the topic, so what I am telling you would be accurate, comprehensive, and helpful for your recovery process. You've been mistreated enough. I want to give you the truth, so you can find your way back to your inner shining beacon of light and love.

During my research, I began to realize that there were many people who had experienced this kind of relationship. I know when I was going through it, I felt incredibly isolated—and you likely do too—but we are not alone. There are many others out there who are finding the courage to free themselves from abusive relationships and tell their stories so others can benefit. For me, it is humbling to see how brave they are.

In these books, I first explain the traits of narcissism and tell you honestly how they manifested in my own relationship. I take you through my story and how I escaped the nightmare of narcissistic abuse. In my second book, I take you through various techniques to help you heal from the emotional—and maybe physical—abuse you've suffered at the hands of your toxic partner.

It is my deepest desire in sharing these experiences and recovery techniques with you that they will help you to heal the wounds so that you can once again hope and dream about finding your perfect life.

This is my wish for you—that you might find the answers you seek in these pages as well as the inspiration to break free and find peace. I understand that you might not feel as though that is possible right now, but I assure you, it is. I, and many others who have gone through this, walk beside you in spirit as you find your way back to that luminous being you once were.

With sincere peace and love,

Elena Miro

Introduction

"Good evening, Elena. Are you and your mom okay with this pandemic situation? I'm worried about you and just need to know you're okay.

After almost two years, I wanted to write to you because I have been thinking about you a lot lately. The power of memories is very profound. What we lived was something unique, and I find myself missing it more and more, missing you more and more… I am sure you will understand my thoughts, but it's important you know that I just can't get you off my mind. I don't know where you are nor what you do, but I know one thing—I think about you all the time.

Dear Elena, I remember everything about you. I hope I will be able to hold you in my arms again soon, my Elena, my 'Shine.'"

His words opened a door to my past that I wasn't sure I wanted to step through. I thought long and hard about the relationship we had, and as I thought about it, I realized that I am not the only one to have experienced the pain of being in love with a narcissist. That thought inspired me to write my story and share it with you. I hope it will save you some pain.

Only two years ago, I was happily married. It seems like it was so much longer ago than that. Incredibly, my life at that time had been completely changed in less than a year, and I remember being so grateful to the universe for giving me this wonderful man. He seemed like the man I had been waiting for my entire life. I thought I was so lucky. But nothing is free. Let me start from the beginning.

I am from Ukraine, and that's where I was when this started. I had not been very satisfied with the dating and relationship experiences I had with Ukrainian men, so I decided to sign up for an international dating website. I had a pretty clear picture in my head of the man I wanted. At the time, I was 31-years-old and on top of my game. I felt like I was at my most beautiful, had plenty of energy, and was an intelligent woman. What's more, I have blonde hair, long legs, and a kind heart. I also had my life together. I had a beautiful apartment, a good car, and my own little business. I'm not boasting here, but it's a relatively attractive setup. In fact, I would describe myself as a dream wife by anyone's standards. So, when my ex—I'll call him Francois—first wrote to me on that dating site, I wasn't really interested in answering him. He was ten years older than me, a Frenchman from Paris, worked for a corporation, and had a kid. He wasn't my type at all.

I never would have imagined myself with a Frenchman. At one point, I even asked him how he felt living in such a big, dirty city that was full of crime. Although Paris is considered the city of love for many people, it wasn't even on my top ten list of destinations to visit, let alone where I wanted to live. So, at first, I had no interest in him, but he certainly had an interest in me. I was his perfect type, and he set his sights on making me part of his second attempt at a family. As it turned out, he saw me as a perfect fit for his beautiful life and knew that with me, he would have a higher status and more respect from his friends and colleagues. That motivated him to pursue me relentlessly.

Francois was very persistent in wooing me. He bombarded me with sweet messages and compliments. I felt like a queen, a goddess—any woman would. He was so sweet, delicate, and polite. He was also so single-minded in achieving his goal of winning me over. I thought, "What a man!" He seemed to know what he wanted and acted immediately to get it. It seemed so masculine and romantic. I would later realize that all of this were potential signs of narcissistic behavior. There are many famous examples of narcissists, and the women who have been with them say they were so charming when they were pursuing the object of their affection—the toy they wanted at the moment.

After only one week of communication, Francois sent me a beautiful bucket of red roses, and he bought a ticket to come to my city and meet me. He had taken to calling me, "my shine." To him, I was light and bright, and strangely, even after two years of being apart, he still calls me that. Everything was going so fast. Francois was active, purposeful, and decisive. I kept thinking he was a confident man who wasn't afraid to go after what he wanted. I was captivated by his masculinity and confident, decisive actions, and he seemed to be backing his words with real action. He was like a rocketman, which became my nickname for him.

For me, it was like a whirlwind of emotions, actions, and surprises, and it seemed that a new chapter of my life was indeed starting. He was eager for our relationship to progress, and he showed it with everything he did. He came to visit me. It was only for two days, but I still remember how nervous and flustered he was at the airport when I met him for the first time. I interpreted it as an indicator of how valuable and important I was to him. Still, I am a strong, smart, modern woman, and I thought it better to put some distance between us until I knew him better. So, we went to a countryside hotel to spend a day there.

By the end of our weekend, I started to look at Francois differently. First, he was in great shape. He had been a surfer since childhood, so he was very fit. I began to see him as a sexy Frenchman. But it wasn't just that. I thought I would surprise him with an uncomfortable question: I asked him what his plan was for us. I thought he might stammer with uncertainty, but instead, he responded immediately. He said he would leave Ukraine the next day and invite me to Paris in two weeks. He told me how much he wanted to show the city to me. He then told me that if everything went well on that visit, the two of us would go on vacation for a week somewhere. A few months after that, he said that he would propose to me, and in one year, he assured me that we would be married.

Again, I was thinking that he was a confident, decisive, masculine man who goes after what he wants. I started thinking, "Maybe this really is my man." That evening, he asked how long I planned on leaving my profile on the dating website. He told me he was going to remove his profile. I know now this was him violating my boundaries, but he wasn't successful. I told him I would think about it and decide on my own since I was officially still single. I was still good at the beginning of our relationship at maintaining firm boundaries. I think now that probably made me even more desirable to him.

When he was leaving, he told me, "I love you," after a short kiss. I remember thinking how strange it was that the French would say these kinds of powerful words after knowing someone for only two days. I couldn't see how that could be true, but he was very convincing. As he left, I told him I would think about his invitation for me to come to Paris.

The next day while doing yoga, I caught myself smiling as I thought about him. I missed him. He seemed so genuine in his affection for me. I even entertained the idea that he was actually in love with me. Who doesn't dream of such a romantic, sweep-you-off-your-feet kind of meeting? At the time, it seemed like a fairy tale. But, like all fairy tales, there is a villain. Sometimes, that villain is disguised. It might look like someone you love and trust, but it's really the big, bad wolf. That's a narcissist: a wolf in sheep's clothing.

Does this sound familiar to you? Have you been charmed by a narcissist only to wake up one day wondering how you could have fallen for their false seductiveness? Well, you're not alone. Like me, you've probably found yourself wondering if they ever really loved you at all. Was it all an act? Is a narcissist even capable of genuine emotions? And, most important of all, how can I regain my own confidence and sense of trust in the universe after having suffered in a relationship with a narcissist?

Answering those questions is why I wanted to write this book. Join me on a journey through my own personal pain and recovery from narcissistic abuse. There is a way to recover, and I'll show you how I did it. I'll take you through each stage of my relationship—from the high-flying honeymoon phase to the realization that I had to get out. I will help you understand the warning signs of your partner potentially being a narcissist and discuss how to heal yourself once you're out of the relationship. I will help you regain your sense of self and your self-confidence. I know I can help you because I've lived through the same nightmare you're experiencing. I understand what you're going through, and I can help you find your way out of the darkness. Let's get started today.

Chapter One: What is Narcissism?

When I first met Francois, I thought he was the perfect man for me. You can likely see why from what I've already shared. He was so sweet and admiring. If you had told me then that he would turn into a crazy monster, I would have not believed you. As it turns out, what I experienced is very common for a narcissist. Like many people, I had no clue about this mental disorder. I never would have imagined that someone so seemingly kind, understanding, and supportive could change so quickly. And, yet, he did; he changed on a dime. Since experiencing this myself, I felt I needed to understand it more. I thought it would help me feel like I could spot it should I encounter it again in the future. A relationship with a narcissist leaves you feeling like you can't trust your own judgment, so for me, learning more about it was something I felt I had to do. If you're reading this book, you must feel the same way, so let's begin with a better understanding of the condition. First, what exactly is narcissism? Is it the same as being selfish or arrogant? As it turns out, it's a lot more complex than that.

Narcissism is something that everyone has a little of if they have healthy self-esteem. Basically, narcissism is on a continuum, and everyone falls somewhere on the spectrum. In healthy doses, narcissism contributes to your confidence, resilience, and ambition. It's only when this personality trait goes to the extremes that it can become pathological.

Among extreme forms of narcissism, known as a narcissistic personality disorder (NPD), studies indicate there are various subtypes that can occur in its expression. Even though the *Diagnostic and Statistical Manual of Mental Disorders* (DSM) blankets narcissism as one homogenous disorder, experts have identified the following basic subtypes:

- **Grandiose narcissism**: This narcissist is arrogant, bold, and well, grandiose. They are often oblivious to their own exploitative acts, lack of empathy, intense aggression, envy, and exhibitionism. They genuinely don't understand they're doing anything wrong or out of the ordinary. Extreme grandiose types are often classified under *malignant narcissism*. Malignant narcissists undermine families and any organizations with which they are involved, and they dehumanize the people in their lives.

- **Vulnerable narcissism**: This type of narcissist is often hypersensitive and exhibits traits of helplessness, defensiveness, hypersensitivity, low self-esteem, shame, and emotional emptiness. These traits manifest outwardly as socially avoidant behavior. In other words, they withdraw whenever social approval is needed and not given.

- **Hypervigilant narcissism**: Similar to the previous type, this narcissist is also overly sensitive and experiences frequent feelings of shame.

- **High-functioning narcissism**: This individual has a less severe expression of NPD and can function as a socially acceptable person in society.

Yet, another study identified five subtypes of narcissist that included the following:

1. **Unprincipled narcissist**: This individual is unscrupulous, amoral, disloyal, fraudulent, deceptive, arrogant, exploitive, domineering, contemptuous, and vindictive. Basically, they're a con artist and a charlatan.

2. **Amorous narcissist**: This individual is sexually seductive, charming, tantalizing, glib, enticing, clever, and bewitching, but they're also pathological liars, swindlers, and disinclined to form any real intimacy.

3. **Compensatory narcissist**: This person offsets their feelings of inferiority and low self-esteem by creating illusions of superiority.

They project an image of being exceptional, admirable, and noteworthy. They derive their self-worth from their efforts of self-enhancement rather than actually doing the work to be admirable.

4. **Elitist narcissist**: This individual feels privileged and empowered because of pseudo-achievements and/or special childhood status. They project an entitled facade that is upwardly mobile and seeks favor in the good life. They try to cultivate a special status by association and seek the advantages that come with that status.

5. **Normal narcissist**: This is the least severe expression of NPD. This individual still feels entitled and deficient in reciprocity, but they are bold in certain environments and often have a higher degree of self-confidence. They are generally competitive and talented in leadership positions, but they feel themselves to be unique and expect recognition from others.

Narcissism and Other Mental Conditions

It's not uncommon for narcissism to be combined with other mental disorders, and this definitely exacerbates both. This was the case for F. He also had a borderline personality disorder, which was a big red flag for reaching any kind of effective resolution within our relationship. It's part of what made his behavior so erratic. That's why it's important to understand how complicated these kinds of mental disorders can become. Let's look at how the various combinations affect the possibility of treatment and the behavior those affected can expect to see.

Borderline Personality Disorder and NPD: In addition to these types, NPD also often co-occurs with a borderline personality disorder. In fact, studies have found that as many as 16 to 39 percent of patients diagnosed with a borderline personality disorder also have NPD. The combination of these two conditions means that the individuals affected will be very resistant to treatment. That's already true for people diagnosed with NPD since they tend to blame everyone else for any problems they have. The co-occurrence of borderline personality disorder just makes treatment even more difficult since those with BPD also don't see that they are the cause of both their and others' suffering. Moreover, people suffering from both conditions are less likely than those who only have one disorder to see an improvement in their symptoms over time.

Bipolar and NPD: There is no recognized link between these conditions, but people in the grips of bipolar mania often display strong narcissistic behaviors like high levels of confidence, feelings of superiority, and grandiose perceptions of self. Furthermore, during depressive states, bipolar individuals may also display other types of narcissistic characteristics. These include avoiding social contact, being insensitive to the needs of others, and neglecting caring duties. The two conditions have such similar symptoms, in fact, that it's possible for them to be confused, and an individual with one condition could easily be diagnosed with the other.

NPD and Addiction: Although people, like Francois, who suffer from NPD may seem like they feel good about themselves, the truth is that their appearance of arrogance masks feelings of shame, helplessness, and uncontrolled rage. Moreover, because their disorder causes destructive behaviors that make it difficult to form meaningful and lasting bonds, they often feel quite isolated and worthless. It's not surprising that many with NPD turn to addictive substances to help them feel relaxed, more comfortable, and give them a sense of belonging. NPD is in Cluster B of personality disorders. These personality disorders are characterized by dramatic, overly emotional, or unpredictable thoughts or behaviors. The research into these problems shows that anyone suffering from such a disorder is at an increased risk for substance abuse.

Link Between NPD and Physical Ailments

On top of everything else that NPD affects negatively, it also adversely affects physical health, particularly for men who suffer from this condition. Even when not stressed, narcissistic men have higher levels of stress hormones in their bloodstream. Those can lead to a whole range of health problems, including an increased risk for cardiovascular disease, obesity, diabetes, depression, gastrointestinal problems, asthma, and high blood pressure. Moreover, because narcissists often turn to substances to numb their pain, they are at a higher risk from adverse health effects resulting from addiction to any number of substances. Lastly, the conflict between a narcissist and health providers due to the sense of superiority exhibited in patients with NPD can often result in noncompliance with treatment regimens, which can increase their risk of death, particularly in patients with long-term illnesses requiring intensive treatment, like cancer.

It is clear that NPD is a dangerous and difficult mental condition to manage, and it will endanger the health of anyone who suffers from it. Furthermore, it's a tough condition to diagnose, which means it can go undiagnosed—thus, untreated—sometimes for a person's entire life, particularly since the individual who has this problem might not recognize they have it at all. Even if they do, they may be unwilling to seek medical diagnosis and treatment. Identifying NPD can be problematic, as it has the many different expressions we've discussed. Even so, there are no pure subtypes of narcissism, and many of the traits described for one of these subtypes, as well as other personality disorders, might also appear in someone with a different disorder. That's part of the problem with separating the multitude of expressions of this mental disorder. Moreover, as my own analyst suggested, it's normal to have some narcissistic traits. Identifying the extreme types of narcissism as distinct from healthy narcissism can be difficult. So, what kinds of behaviors indicate normal narcissism, and what would be defined as extreme? Let's take a look.

Healthy Narcissism

After seeking psychological help for the abuse I endured in my relationship with a narcissist, I told my analyst that I would be writing a book about narcissism based on my love story, and she said, "Will you write that you are narcissistic as well?"

That shocked me, but I soon realized that it didn't necessarily mean I had NPD; I do, however, harbor some narcissistic traits. I noted the common features I share with narcissists as I was studying the condition. Of course, I'm not the kind of monster that manipulates people, but I definitely have some features of narcissism. It's also frequently true that narcissists are attracted to one another, and we live in a narcissistic society, but is everyone a *narcissist?*

In fact, most people are to some degree because some narcissism is necessary for healthy self-esteem. It's normal for hard-working people to crave approval; that's a need that is driven by ego, and it serves to help you feel loved, unique, valuable, important, powerful, successful, and in charge of your life. Moreover, most people naturally try to avoid criticism and feelings of inferiority, but a healthy dose of constructive criticism and some feelings of inferiority drive us to take action, so we can feel a sense of power and control over our lives. This is a natural and healthy drive since it helps protect us from failing and severe disappointments. In short, a good dose of narcissism is a powerful force that helps us better ourselves. The traits of healthy narcissism include the following:

- **Self-awareness**: If you have a healthy dose of narcissism, you are quiet and comfortably confident. You know both your strengths and shortcomings, and you see how both are essential parts of your wholeness. You know you're not perfect, and you don't have an expectation that you will be perfect. You view yourself as constantly growing and learning, and you see no need to compare yourself to others.

- **Collaborative**: Healthy narcissists are collaborative because they have a mature sense of self-confidence, and they know they will get their needs met without having to put others down or keep them from achieving their goals. As a healthy narcissist, you are able to engage in mutually satisfying relationships with other people. You don't lose yourself in their opinions, you don't allow yourself to be pressured to be like them, and you can maintain your sense of self.

- **Earn approval**: A healthy dose of narcissism results in approval that is earned rather than from any sense of entitlement. You know that you have to work hard to achieve your goals, and if there is a failure or setback, you trust that it doesn't have to do so much with your ability as with a need to either work harder or receive more training. You're not resentful of having to work hard; in fact, it inspires you. Additionally, you have no problem asking for help or more information when you need it.

- **Flexibility**: Healthy narcissists are flexible rather than rigid or controlling. They have no need to control others, and they make for excellent negotiators and problem solvers. Their goal is to get things done in a way that benefits everyone involved. They can work healthily as part of a team without feeling that their ego has been deflated. They can withstand setbacks and changes in plans, something those with an unhealthy expression of narcissism simply cannot abide.

- **Firm**: Healthy narcissism also means knowing when to stand firm. If you have a healthy dose of narcissism, you have no problem setting and maintaining firm boundaries or saying no, and you don't tolerate bullies, discourteous treatment, or devious motives. You stand firm in your authenticity and integrity and have an unshakable concept of self. You know your worth, are confident in your abilities, and don't compromise your values.

- **Respectful**: One of the biggest differences between healthy and unhealthy narcissism is treating others with respect. Even when you disagree with someone, if you're a healthy narcissist, you discuss the issue respectfully and without resorting to insults or bullying. You understand that nothing is black and white; there is always a gray area. You also have a good dose of self-respect, so you don't tolerate condescension from people who believe themselves to be superior to you. You know they are not superior and neither are you; you are both genuine and humble in your behavior and treatment of others.

- **Unselfish**: This is another area where the difference between a healthy narcissist and an unhealthy one is particularly notable. Healthy narcissists are not selfish. They enjoy helping when they can, work hard, and care about the welfare of others. They make great team players because they care about the success of the team as much as their own personal success. They seek to help their family achieve their goals, even if it means they must sacrifice for that to happen. They are willing to do so because they understand that it's not all about them, and they want to see their family members succeed.

- **Emotionally intelligent**: Healthy narcissists maintain a positive mindset, even when they are faced with challenges in life. They control their baser impulses and think before they speak. They stay mindful and ground themselves in the present, so they can sense the emotions around them and understand their own feelings and sensations clearly.

These are the main traits of healthy narcissism. It basically comes down to a balance. Too little narcissism leads to a lack of self-esteem and self-confidence, resulting in a fearful state of mind that interferes with success. Too much narcissism creates a bully—someone who is overly selfish and manipulative and compromises social cohesion to stand out. That's exactly what I would experience with F. I couldn't believe it as I watched my "perfect man" turn into a childish, needy, and angry monster. You see, the right balance is key, but let's look at unhealthy narcissism and how it can manifest in the people you love.

Narcissistic Personality Disorder (NPD)

Any personality trait that is taken to the extreme can become pathological. Someone who is excessively narcissistic can be diagnosed with NPD. Someone with a normal amount of narcissism can sometimes be self-centered, but for a person with NPD, this is a pervasive pattern of behavior. The reality is that someone who has NPD has an extremely fragile ego and low self-esteem, which they mask with an inflated sense of superiority. Their insecurity is so bad that it interferes with their functioning in society. It has also been shown that people with NPD have less brain matter in the areas of the brain associated with empathy, so they quite simply cannot see your side of anything and have no interest in seeing that your needs are met.

It's not unusual for people to assume someone is a narcissist because they don't like that person. So, how can you tell if someone is *really* a narcissist? To be diagnosed with NPD, the DSM requires that the following criteria be met:

- Excessive need for approval and admiration;
- A sense of entitlement, condescending behavior, and a belief in one's superiority;
- A lack of empathy and the inability to recognize the needs of other people;
- Superficial relationships;
- Dramatic mood swings.

Remember that only a professional can make an official diagnosis on someone; nevertheless, you can use these points as a starting point for your own diagnosis. These criteria should remain relatively stable across time and in different social settings for a diagnosis. Note that these traits cause a number of unhealthy, manipulative behaviors in the narcissist. I experienced the manifestation of these criteria in numerous social settings. It was really surreal. I would never have believed that my loving man would act that way toward me and the people around us. No one was immune to his nasty temper. To understand this more, let's discuss some common manipulations that narcissists use to get you under their control. You'll be surprised at how insidious some of these tactics are, and you may not want to believe them, but if you think about how you're being treated, you might begin to see some similarities.

10 Common Narcissistic Manipulations

So, how does a pathological narcissist act, specifically? Although there are different subcategories of narcissism, these toxic people share several behaviors in common. In general, they seek to exploit, demean, and hurt intimate partners, family members, and friends. They use a variety of manipulative techniques to distort the reality of their victims and do it excessively while they try to avoid being accountable for their actions. Francois was an expert at this. He had me questioning my own sanity after a while. The following is a list of specific techniques they can use to distort your reality:

1. **Gaslighting**: Gaslighting is an insidious technique designed to make you feel as though you're crazy. Basically, the narcissist will insist that you imagined something that you claim really did happen. This is one of the main ways toxic people work to distort your reality. It can quietly eat away at your trust in your judgment. It can eventually cause you to stop calling out abuse and mistreatment because you question if you're just imagining the situation. It takes someone strongly grounded in their own reality to resist this technique. This came to be a favorite technique for Francois, and he did have me questioning my own judgment. It's particularly harmful because unless you have

34

someone who can help you see the truth, you really do feel like you're losing it.

2. **Projection**: Toxic people always project their shortcomings onto the people around them. They will do anything to avoid being held accountable. It's a defense mechanism they use to avoid ownership. Although most people project to some extent, the narcissist is psychologically abusive in the manner of their projection. They are frequently painful and cruel in the manner they do this. They actively try to make their loved ones feel ashamed for something that is not even their own shortcoming. It's a way they can shift the blame from themselves to someone else. It has the effect of distorting reality and creating self-doubt in their victims. Francois was a master projector. He was always accusing me of the very thing he was doing or that something bad was happening to him. It was insane!

3. **Nonsensical conversations**: Toxic people, like malignant narcissists, will often use a variety of techniques over the course of a conversation to distort reality. It's almost impossible to have a thoughtful discussion with a narcissist. Instead, it becomes a nonsensical word salad with circular arguments, projection, and gaslighting all

rolled into one. It's a tactic designed to cause frustration and confusion, and most of all, distract you from the main problem about which you were talking. They also want to make you feel guilty for even having your own thoughts and opinions, especially if they differ from their own. For you, the result is that you start to wonder how the argument began in the first place. The truth is it began because your disagreement threatened their sense of omniscience and superiority. These toxic people thrive on drama, so anything you have to say in the argument just becomes more fuel for their craziness.

4. **Blanket statements**: Many narcissists are intellectually lazy, relying instead on their ability to distort reality rather than actually considering your side of the argument. For that reason, they have a tendency to generalize anything and everything you say. They don't take into account the nuances of your arguments; they simply dismiss your perspective altogether. They also use blanket generalizations to invalidate experiences that don't fit with their beliefs. For them, it helps maintain the status quo. For example, if you were to say that a narcissist's behavior is unacceptable, they might reply that you're always too sensitive. Although you might be too sensitive sometimes, it can also be true

that your narcissistic abuser is insensitive and cruel most of the time. They're simply generalizing a partial truth to the extent that it undermines your argument.

5. **Absurdly misrepresenting your thoughts**: Toxic people do what they can to make their loved ones appear absurd or even malicious. Toward that end, they often translate your different opinions, legitimate emotions, and lived experiences into character flaws or even evidence of your irrational nature. If you express your feelings, you might hear your narcissistic abuser respond with something like, "Oh, now you're perfect, huh?" They use this kind of sentiment to invalidate your right to have your own thoughts and emotions, and they also want to cause you to feel guilty if you attempt to establish boundaries. They will also jump to conclusions about what you're thinking or feeling when they get triggered by what you're saying. They will put words in your mouth and depict you as being outlandish or having nefarious intentions. This is another form of cognitive distortion designed to keep you off guard. Their ultimate goal is to convince you that you should be ashamed if you try to give them realistic feedback.

6. **Nitpicking and moving the goal**: Toxic narcissists nitpick and scapegoat you every chance they get. They don't really want to help you, so they're not offering constructive criticism. Instead, they're trying to pull you down. They combine this technique with moving the goal as a means of justifying their perpetual dissatisfaction with you. If you showed them proof of what you're saying or met their demands, they set up more expectations or demand more proof. If you even come close to meeting their demands, the goal will change. By changing and raising the expectations consistently, they can instill a sense of unworthiness in their victims. They will never feel as if you are doing enough to make them happy. It can also make you hyper-focused on trying to please the narcissist, which is exactly what they want you to do: question yourself to the point of obsession. In the end, it's all for naught, because even if you do bend over backwards to try to please them, it won't change the horrific way they treat you.

7. **Changing the subject**: This is another favored tactic for the narcissist. They will change the subject, so they can't be held accountable for any problem. If you're talking about something they did today, they will bring up something you did two years ago as a

diversion. They often start with, "What about when you…" This can have the effect of derailing the conversation, and of course, if they're successful in that, the issue won't be resolved, and they cannot be held accountable for their actions.

8. **Covert and overt threats**: If you challenge a narcissist's sense of entitlement, the false sense of superiority, or grandiose sense of self in any way, they will often respond with overt or covert threats. They will try to make you fearful of the consequences for disagreeing with their demands. Any challenge to their perceived sense of superiority will result in an ultimatum: "Do this or I'll do that." It doesn't really matter what the "that" is—whether it's leaving you or a physical threat, these threats are a huge red flag that someone feels entitled to where they don't believe they should have to compromise. You should take threats very seriously by documenting them, particularly if they're threats of physical violence, and you should also follow up by reporting such threats, so there is a record of the incident.

9. **Name-calling**: This is another way that narcissists and other toxic people can distract from the issue at hand. They like to strike out preemptively at anything they perceive as threatening to their sense of superiority and

entitlement. They are the only ones in the conversation who can be right, and someone who challenges them may fall victim to their narcissistic rage. In this state, they often resort to name-calling because they can't come up with a better way to manipulate your opinions and manage your emotions. It's a quick and easy way to degrade you and invalidate your right to have your own thoughts and emotions. No matter how well-researched or informed your opinion, the name-calling tactic quickly casts it as a sill or idiotic. The narcissist uses this tactic because they can't come up with a convincing rebuttal to your argument, so they have to target you personally to undermine your credibility.

10. **Destructive conditioning**: This is where a toxic person conditions you to associate your strengths, talents, and even your happy memories with abuse. They use covert and overt insults about the very qualities they once admired in you to demean you and sabotage your goals. They also use this tactic to ruin your celebrations as well as your vacations and holidays. They can also use this technique to isolate you from your friends and family, and it can also work to make you financially dependent on them. As was the case with Pavlov's dog which was conditioned to salivate at the sound of a bell, you become

conditioned to avoid using your talents to make your own life fulfilling. They do this so that you won't outshine them. They also believe that everything you do should be related to pleasing them. Additionally, they don't want something other than them to have any control over your life. To them, their influence over you is the most important thing, and they are, therefore, pathologically envious. Moreover, if you achieve success and happiness that is unrelated to them, they are jealous since they can't find that inner joy. Finally, if you can find validation outside of them, then what will keep you from leaving them? I know this was particularly worrisome for Francois. He never wanted me to outshine him. It got to the point he didn't want me to dress up since others might look at me instead of him. He used this technique to ruin each of our vacations, including our honeymoon!

My narcissistic abuser employed most, if not all, of these techniques plus a few I'll mention later on. If you think you're in a relationship with a toxic partner, you likely recognize these tactics too. Still, if you think you're in love with that person, you might be wondering what causes NPD and if it is treatable.

Causes and Treatment of NPD

The precise causes of narcissism are unknown, but experts believe it likely has both a genetic and environmental link. It's quite possible that the condition forms in childhood in the case of inconsistent or inadequate parenting – parents who were either too indulgent or too critical during the formative years. In Francois's case, his mother once told me that when he was 6 months old, she had to leave him for a month to help his father who was working in Africa. It was an emergency situation, and it required that she stop breastfeeding suddenly. When she returned, she said that Francois was hugging her nonstop. He was also crying, trembling, and he became very clingy, refusing to let her go anywhere without him.

People used to think that children that young weren't affected much by trauma like that, but psychologists now understand that during the first two years of life, we form our basic understanding of the world as safe or unsafe. If we determine it to be an unsafe place where our needs might not always be met, it's possible to develop problems attaching to people and forming meaningful relationships later in life. That can be disastrous for any intimate relationships we might have. For a narcissist like Francois, not only are romantic partnerships affected by their inability to form healthy relationships, but they also can't raise emotionally healthy children. I witnessed first hand how the children of narcissists suffer phobias themselves due to a lack of real love and closeness they need. In fact, as they are exposed to the high expectations, endless comparisons, and the manipulative behaviors of their narcissistic parents, they often become narcissists themselves. It's a sad story, and I feel for Francois and his daughter, I really do, but my own self-esteem is solid enough that I won't sacrifice myself for someone who is abusive, even if his mental problems resulted from his own sad childhood experiences. Neither should you.

As for treatments, it is absolutely necessary to prevent or repair the damage done to their interpersonal relationships. *The condition is not curable*, but it can be treated. Treatment, however, requires a lot of time and much patience. It often involves multiple forms of psychotherapy, including individual, group, and family therapies, and it takes years to see improvements. The research does suggest that empathy can be learned, but it will take time for the individual to accept responsibility for their actions and better understand how they affect the people in their lives. To work at all though, the narcissist must be aware of their problem—which is often almost impossible—and they need to be ready to work on it. It's also important to realize that narcissism combines frequently with other personality disorders. This was the situation in my case. Francois was a psychopathic narcissist. That would require even more time for treatment. It's not a very hopeful picture because during that time, you'll be suffering from their abusive behavior. Still, there is hope, but if you're considering staying with your abuser, you'll need to set firm boundaries and be rock solid in understanding your self-worth. You'll also need to have a Plan B, just in case.

If all of this sounds like a nightmare, I can assure you it is, and if you're living through it, it may feel impossible to escape. My heart cries for you because I know the helpless, hopeless, and confusing feelings you're experiencing. However, know that there is hope, as my story will show you. I understand what this feels like and want to help you by telling you what I went through—how I fell in love with this person, how I realized what I was dealing with, and how I escaped and recovered from the abuse. Let me share my journey with you.

Chapter Two: Prince Charming—Beware the Charming Narcissist

My initial meeting with Francois did sweep me off my feet. He was so charming. Of course, I agreed to go to Paris, and in less than two weeks, I was landing in what many consider the most romantic city in the world. All my female friends were dying from envy. It was never my dream city, but because I am a girl who loves romance and everything connected to love, after Francois met me at the airport with flowers, I found that my heart was beating faster when I got into his car.

My Prince Charming

From that moment on, it was like a dream. After dropping my things off at my hotel room, we went on his motorbike to Parisian Chinatown for lunch. I was starving after the flight, but that was momentarily forgotten as I was sitting behind him on the bike and looking around at the "City of Lights." I thought to myself, "Baby, it's Paris. You might not have dreamed about coming here, but here you are!" It was so surrealistic—riding behind this man on the bike, the wind whipping through my hair. I was smiling at what seemed like the beginning of a modern fairy tale. I knew this weekend would decide the fate of our love story. Either we would begin our journey together, or I would continue my search alone.

That evening, we went to the Eiffel Tower. I took a picture there and sent it to my mom. You could see how genuinely happy I was in that photo. The next day, Francois took me on a tour of the city. We went walking through town and visited famous historical sights. I was mesmerized by the beautiful Notre Dame de Paris Cathedral. I nearly cried as I walked through this world-renowned cathedral. As a child, I had read the romanticist Victor Hugo's famous novel, *The Hunchback of Notre-Dame*, and now I was here seeing what he had brought to life in my young imagination. I danced in the yard of the Louvre Museum and took pictures in front of the Champs-Élysées with the Triumph Arc just behind me. It was like a beautiful, romantic dream. How could I not fall in love?

Later, we went to the best restaurant in Paris. There were some famous people as well. I felt like a princess in my sexy, elegant navy dress with an open back and my red Louboutin shoes. My long, blond hair was styled in waves and laying softly on my shoulders. I could see how attracted Francois was to me as he looked at me. I noted how pleased he was to see people watching me as I walked to the restroom. And, I definitely sashayed. If there's one thing I know, it's how to walk in high heels in a royal, elegant manner. It seemed like the perfect night, and I knew that a new chapter in my life was starting. I could tell I was Francois's dream woman, and I was beginning to think he was my dream man.

We also made love that night. Francois was stressed and nervous, so it was a bit awkward, but it signaled our intentions to pursue this relationship. As we sat on his bed, hugging and kissing, we both realized we were in love. I felt as though my spirit was soaring. I returned home to Ukraine feeling like a new woman. I was so blissfully happy. I couldn't wait to see him again.

Two weeks later, he came to Ukraine again, just for the weekend. We went to a countryside hotel with a spa and had a wonderful time together. We even started talking about having kids. Our relationship was progressing at light speed. It was full of romance—flowers, gifts, and love weekends—just like a movie. I couldn't believe how happy I felt. It was hard to part again, but we knew we would see each other in another week. We had planned a trip to the Canary Islands. Neither of us had been there, and it's a great place for surfing, which was Francois's hobby. It would be our first real trip together.

Red Flags…?

The next week, I flew to Paris and the next day, we left for Santa Cruz. Francois was nervous and very stressed at the airport. He explained that he didn't like that part of a vacation since, as a child, his mother would get stressed by traveling and yell at him and his brother. He said she would throw luggage and yell at them every time they went on vacation. I had a much different experience as a child. My family struggled with money and health issues, so I never even dared dream about going on a trip that involved flying. For me, flying was an exciting experience. Aside from my natural optimism, it feels like a special treat, since we could never do it when I was young.

To me, it wasn't about the travel experience itself as much as it was about the person I was sharing the experience with, but Francois clearly didn't see it that way. What's more, his mood would swing from rage to joy in the blink of an eye. It was shocking to me. I had never experienced that kind of dramatic mood swing before. I tried to calm him down when I could. For example, we got stuck in a traffic jam after a short trip to the Vulcano, and I tried to distract him by reading about the history of Tenerife island. It was like he was a little child. I started to wonder where the nice, polite, kind man I thought I was coming to know was?

I'm a naturally positive person. Life has taught me to look on the bright side, so it was hard for me to understand why he couldn't enjoy our time together, even if we were in a traffic jam. I didn't know this was part of a larger pattern yet. The next day, we had a trip to the ocean planned. Francois wanted to try a fly board. The ocean helped him release stress as did a little burst of adrenaline whenever he tried a new adventure. This was something I would come to understand later. He liked the ocean so much that I started calling him "my fish." He loved that nickname, and I loved him. That's why I didn't understand why he was in such a foul mood that morning. I chose to ignore it, but he was making it difficult.

He was obstinate like a child as he resisted the fly board experience. He said angrily that he didn't want to do the fly board and maybe he would try it next time.

"But why? What is going on, my fish? You have to try it. Please, for me? I want to see how you master this fly board with your professional surf skills," I implored.

51

He agreed, since he was doing it for me. It was a joy for him, too. As I watched him on the fly board, I thought it was like a little boy playing with a new toy. As the adrenaline rush from his new experience washed away his foul mood, the pleasure he found in the adventure—and a little shot of oxytocin, a feel-good hormone—made him feel better. He was once again full of joy and excitement, like a kid… and it was then that I learned the true reason for his bad mood.

He said, "You know, this morning I was angry at you because you didn't give me a blow job, but after the fly board, I'm not angry at you anymore."

I was stunned. I hadn't even known he wanted a blow job. He hadn't said anything, but he had certainly judged me as guilty. In this behavior, Francois demonstrated two other common tactics of narcissistic abusers. He was shaming me basically for not reading his mind and knowing what he wanted. He had an unrealistic expectation that I would somehow intuit what he wanted, and when I didn't, he became angry and tried to shame me for not recognizing his desire. It's an insidious technique designed to keep you on edge all the time trying to please your partner. It's also related to yet another technique the abusive narcissist will use: control. If Francois could be successful in having me always thinking about his needs so I wouldn't miss something he wanted, he would have much more control over me.

Despite my shock—along with a little, nagging worry that was starting to creep into the corners of my mind—I didn't want to spoil our vacation. I was so in love, and I refused to let anything get in the way of our burgeoning relationship. At that time, I had no idea what a narcissist was or how they acted. I remember now that he even said to me one time that he was a narcissist. I remember thinking that he must mean he pays a lot of attention to his appearance. To me, that was normal for a Frenchman.

Over the course of the next two months, we saw each other every two weeks. He would come to visit me, and I would go visit him. Our relationship was developing as planned, and although I noticed his sudden mood changes, and they were shocking to me, I dismissed them or made excuses. I was in love. I didn't want to see any problems. I wanted to believe in the fairy tale I thought I was living in.

A Few Clues

Around Christmas, I went to Paris again. We were planning on spending the holidays with his mother and daughter. I was anxious to meet his mother. She was a 73-year old, strong woman who had made a career as a doctor while raising two sons alone. She had a difficult, challenging life, but she pushed through. She had also grown up without a father. She was half Vietnamese and half French—her father was a French ambassador in Vietnam who left his family for other women.

"I'm Madame Sofie," she said as she extended her hand to greet me.

She was delighted to see her son so full of energy and optimism with me. She liked me, but I could tell there was something she wasn't telling me. Francois's first marriage had been a long one—almost 15 years. They divorced after she had an affair with her boss in the law firm where she worked. They had a child together and shared custody of her equally. She was 13 years old when I met her. I remember Francois's mother telling me how his ex-wife was always sad and never smiled. At the time, I thought she must be a pessimistic woman, but I would come to understand her reasons for having such an unhappy attitude.

His mother liked me in part because she thought I made her son calm. I thought that was a compliment, but I later understood he was just wearing a mask. As I learned more about his relationship with his mother, I came to believe she was a narcissist too. Every time they were together, they ended up in a shouting match, then she would give him the silent treatment after we left until I melted his heart, and we would visit her again. She lived about 100 km from Paris, so it was a bit of a trip to go visit. It was a real effort that I had to make to bring them together. I didn't want to think he was like her, but I began to see some similarities, and as I mentioned, some researchers do believe there is a genetic link to the disorder.

Just before Christmas, we went to the supermarket to pick up some things. He didn't like supermarkets—too many people and long lines made him crazy. On this occasion, he got so stressed that he ended up throwing the food down inside the supermarket and storming out. I was mortified. I felt so ashamed of my adult man who was behaving like a psychopathic child. I had never seen him so angry and overwhelmed by negative emotions. I stayed silent as we both left the market—he with his rage and me with my shame. I couldn't believe a man of mine was acting this way.

Even after we left the supermarket, he was still angry. My patience ran out, and I told him that it was enough. He needed to stop complaining. With that, I became the new target of his rage, and that's how our first big fight started. From my point of view, I just loved being with him. It didn't matter if we were just going to the supermarket together, the important thing was that we were together. I'm an optimist, so I try to find the good things in my life. I try not to pay attention to the negative things that happen. After so many years of failed romances, I thought I had finally met "The One," and that seemed like a miracle to me. I had even started to love France, and now every time I saw the city from the window of the plane, my heart beat faster with excitement. Every night, before falling asleep, I had been sending out gratitude to the universe for sending me this wonderful man. I thought I could finally have the family I'd been dreaming about, and now, it seemed it was all falling apart. How could this man become so enraged over such a small thing, especially when the woman you love is right next to you?

I told him that I didn't understand his actions, how it made me feel like I was losing my dream, and that I couldn't have this kind of drama in my life anymore. I said it all with tears in my eyes, and when he saw that, he apologized and hugged me. He saw my tears as confirmation of my love for him. It was the first time I shed a tear because of him, but it wouldn't be the last. After our fight, he was so kind and excited. He was using yet another narcissist technique: love bombing. He was positively *smothering* me with affection. It was weird because it seemed like my tears gave him power and improved his self-esteem. Not only that, but my just being his girlfriend was raising his status. His friends were constantly complimenting him for having me. They would tell him I looked like a top model. He saw that as reflecting his own greatness, and it did more than that for him. Because of his increased self-esteem, he soon received a promotion at work and a big raise. He was so proud to have me next to him. Still, he needed me to compliment him as well. He needed recognition and veneration from everyone.

Although having me as a girlfriend was doing wonders for him, Francois still couldn't possess me. I was still independent living in Ukraine. We spent the new year in the mountains. We were so happy and in love. His mother and daughter came with us, and they had a great time too. It seemed that life was great—we were in love, the sex was great, and our future was looking bright. On the day we returned from the mountains, we parked closc to the apartment to unload the car. I noticed a nice sports car in front of us and was intrigued to learn what kind of car it was. It has a symbol of Ukraine on it, and I wanted to know who was inside.

I went to see whose car it was, and this made Francois very nervous. He was practically begging me not to go. He seemed to think there might be a man who owned it, and he didn't want me to talk to him. I didn't listen to him, and I'm glad I didn't. I met my friend Ira that day. She was from Ukraine and was also married to a French man. What's more, they lived just five minutes from where we did. We talked to Ira for about 15 minutes. It was such an easy conversation, so we exchanged phone numbers. Francois and I returned to the apartment, and as soon as we did, he sat on our bed and started to cry. He was holding his head in his hands, sobbing.

"Why are you crying, my love?" I asked.

"You can't believe how my life changed with you. I'm alive again. I saw how easy and natural you were talking with Ira," he told me through his tears.

I stroked his hair to help calm him down. Something so normal for me was so unique to him: closeness with other people and the ability to be genuine and open with them. That's something narcissists can never have. I didn't know that then, though. Instead, I was touched by his emotions and thought it showed just how sensitive and deep he was. It deepened my love for him. I started to think about how difficult it was to keep going back and forth from Ukraine to Paris. Half of my wardrobe was in France and the other half in Ukraine, and then there was my business. It was very slow, and I had been thinking that if I moved to Paris, I would shut it down.

As I thought about it, I realized that I had the family of my dreams, so why not commit to a new life in a new country? I started to learn French and I began watching French movies to learn more about the language and culture. Every time I was in Paris, I explored more of the beautiful city as I visited shops and museums. I even started buying croissants with my morning coffee. I wanted to embrace the French life fully… his life. I wanted to cook French food, understand French jokes, and be the best French woman for my French man. As I look back on it, I think I might have tried too hard. I treated him like he was a king. I was also getting to know him better and could "read" him. In fact, I knew when he was choosing a diamond ring for me, the one he would give me when he proposed sharing our lives together.

Research into the Charming Narcissist

I was totally in love with this man. He seemed so great in every way. At this point, you might be wondering how it is that a narcissist—someone suffering from a mental disorder—can seem that great in the early stages of a relationship. You're not alone; I also wondered the same thing. It turns out that it's not at all unusual. In fact, psychologists will tell you that self-absorbed people can often be very charming at first glance. They seem to hang on your every word and appear to think that what you're saying is important. They focus on you, looking into your eyes and smiling as if you're the best thing since sliced bread. They will also agree with your opinions, compliment you, and even make you feel cherished. In truth, it isn't any wonder that you can fall so deeply in love with a narcissist. It can seem as though you've found your soulmate. I know that's how I felt about Francois.

The trouble is that the very behavioral and physical traits that cause the narcissist to seem so great at first are what are so detrimental to the relationship in the long-run. In fact, one study (Back et al., 2010) found that narcissists produce physical, nonverbal, and verbal cues that indicate attractiveness, competence, interpersonal warmth, and humor to the individual with whom they're interacting. That causes the person to reinforce the narcissist's perception of themselves by complimenting them, and the admiration supports their viewpoint that they are superior. However, because the narcissist produces these cues out of their sense of entitlement and desire to manipulate others, they can't sustain those initial positive behaviors, and your favorable first impression of them won't last. As the relationship goes on, the narcissist begins to betray their true nature. That includes a number of red flags that you would start to notice after a short time:

- A withdrawal of interest in you;
- Interrupting when you're talking and changing the subject;
- Looking around rather than looking at you;
- Ignoring or challenging your opinions, even those with which they previously agreed;
- Criticizing you for small things;
- Rejecting your suggestions;
- Keeping the conversation focused on them;
- Spending less time with you;
- Blaming you for anything and everything they perceive as wrong;

- Showing interest in or complimenting someone else.

These red flags can certainly cause you to become disquieted, but as in my situation with Francois, I couldn't quite put my finger on what was bothering me about him. I knew I didn't like it when he became so stressed and I had to try to calm him down, but I accepted his excuses or made excuses for him because he seemed so perfect otherwise. But that's part of the pattern too. You might experience any or all of the following behaviors and feelings yourself when the narcissist's true nature becomes more apparent:

- Feeling apprehensive about the relationship;
- Making excuses for their behavior;
- Feeling inadequate and that you're unable to please the person;
- Redoubling your efforts to attract them, but it doesn't work;
- Trying to empathize with the person to understand their needs better;
- Violating your own values to keep their attention and interest;
- Confronting them about the changes in their behavior, which usually results in making you feel like you're the one who's got a problem.

Despite your best efforts, nothing seems to work, and that just results in more frustration. The situation leaves you with few choices, and the worst part is, you often start to blame yourself for their problems. It doesn't help to know that they had a narcissistic mother, as Francois did, or that they've been in other relationships that didn't last, or even knowing that they have a mental disorder—none of that really helps because you just become devastated that the person you thought was "the one" isn't at all what they first appeared to be. Instead, they're like a wolf in sheep's clothing, and as much as you don't want to believe that's true, the truth will come out. Let me tell you how it happened for me.

Chapter Three: The Honeymoon Stage—A Psychopath in Sheep's Clothing

On February 14, I dressed to the nines—red dress, red lipstick, and hair styled beautifully in the salon next to our apartment. I was ready for a fantastic Valentine's Day. We were going to visit Notre Dame de Paris Cathedral, a place I had loved since childhood. As so frequently occurred now, Francois became a bit stressed when our taxi was caught up in traffic. It took almost an hour to get to the Notre Dame Cathedral. I was holding his hand to calm him down.

The Engagement

I knew what was coming that night. He had been talking all month about proposing to me, so it wasn't a surprise when he put his left knee on the ground. I still remember his exact words:

"I'm so happy that you appeared in my life and changed it for the best. I love you and my life with you. I promise to be the best husband and always protect you. Will you marry me, Elena?" he said.

How could I possibly say no? I think every girl would dream about that kind of proposal. The ring was simple but beautiful with a large, round diamond. I was so proud to have it on my finger. My mother was ecstatic and happy for me. It truly felt like a fairy tale. I couldn't have dreamed it better. In fact, I kept pinching myself thinking I would wake up, and it all would have been nothing more than a dream. Everything was perfect. I was waking up each morning in Paris, the city of love. I was in bed with my future husband. We had wonderful sex together. He was a great lover for me, and I couldn't believe my luck. Everything was as I dreamt. I always thought before, "I can't be so happy; it's impossible"

My life was not an easy one. I had to survive alone and fight my way to success. My first love and marriage ended in betrayal and left me hating men. Eventually, I recovered from it and forgave him and myself. I was looking forward to starting over and leaving the past behind. Still, after one divorce, it wasn't easy to open my heart and let someone else in. I had finally opened it for Francois; however, there was still that nagging doubt—that feeling that something wasn't right. I just couldn't put my finger on it, but I just sensed that my future would not be what I had hoped. I kept thinking that I lived in what appeared to be a perfect world, though it was merely an illusion.

The Planning

I didn't have time to ponder it much, though, as our next few months were filled with travel and wedding preparations. We spent all Francois's vacation time visiting several countries. Every two months, we were in another exotic location: Martinique, Bali, Spain, and of course, all around France. He needed to surf to release stress and get away from the pressure of his work. His career was skyrocketing. With me, he felt more confident than ever, and that showed in his productivity and decisiveness at work.

On one of our trips, we visited his mother. She gave me a family heirloom: a ring. It was very old, in platinum with two diamonds. I was touched that they trusted me so much. I am well aware of the stereotype that Ukrainian women are looking to marry foreigners for their money, and it meant a great deal to me that she could see I really loved her son and wanted to have a family with him. I still have respect for this woman, even though I know she caused trauma for her son, and I know it is that trauma that still prevents him from creating a long-lasting and fulfilling relationship. In hindsight, I think she knows that. I remember her telling me that he needs to surf as much as possible. It was something she told me while we were having coffee one day. I thought at the time that it was strange advice, but later I realized he needed it as a way to handle the high level of adrenaline he constantly had in his blood. Surfing helped him deal with that, so he could stay calm and positive. If he had no outlet, he got agitated and became likely to explode at everything and everybody.

One example of this was an incident that occurred as we were returning from Bali. We spent two wonderful weeks there, at his villa. At the airport, he found out that the air company was charging him more than he had expected for his surfboards. He erupted. He started shouting at the managers and hurling insults in a fit of rage. He even kicked the wall with his feet. He was acting like a psychopath! He had been in a bad mood on the return flight. Everything was irritating him, and he responded by throwing things and complaining. Finding out about the surfboards was just the last straw that broke the proverbial camel's back. It was the longest return flight of my life. I couldn't wait to get out of the airport. I didn't know where to hide and was so ashamed by his behavior. I had tried to placate him on the flight. I was asking the flight attendant for water, pills, ice (for his feet), napkins, anything to get him to calm down. Still, his bad behavior continued, and it was hard to tolerate.

When we finally got home from that nightmare trip, he parked himself on the sofa and began to watch movies, one after the other. I knew by that point that it was something that relaxed him. By evening, I couldn't stay cooped up in the apartment anymore. I wanted to go to the nearest cafe to get some air and have a little bite to eat. When I asked him to go, he responded by shouting brusquely, "Do I have a right to simply watch TV on my weekend? Why are you bothering me? I'm doing nothing wrong here!" Here is yet another favorite tactic the narcissist uses: condescension. Francois acted like he was so entitled to whatever he wanted, whenever he wanted it, and he felt I should simply know it. The fact that I didn't, brought on his, "I'm so tired of having to explain things to you," tone of voice. There was no trace of the loving man I thought I knew in that voice.

I could see that my sweet husband had checked out, so I put on my sunglasses and left crying, alone. Sometimes, I felt so lonely. If he was in a good mood, he wanted to be with me, but like a toy he had grown tired of, if he was in a bad mood, he wanted nothing to do with me. Over time, he began to shout at me like he did at strangers. What's more was that he started to blame me for everything, and I began to feel guilty too.

Another red flag I noticed was that Francois would start saying that after our wedding, our "real life" would start. To me, that was odd, since I thought it had been real before we got married, and I knew I wouldn't change afterward. But he had a different idea in his head. I think he thought that once we were married, I would be like his property. I might have had an inkling about that, but I couldn't believe it at the time. I didn't want to believe it. I wanted to believe in honesty and pure love. Still, there were things to come that I simply couldn't ignore.

When we went to Ukraine to get the papers I needed to apply for a visa in France, Francois began complaining about a constant pain in his hips. We were staying in a nice countryside hotel, and each day, we would take walks in the forest and visit the spa. Despite the spa treatments, he had this constant pain. When we returned to Paris, he went for an MRI and was diagnosed with arthrosis. The doctors told him he would need new hip joints on both sides. If he didn't get new ones, the pain would progress to where he could become completely unable to walk. He was told not to surf anymore and plan for an operation.

We had already booked a vacation to Biarritz, and there was no way he wasn't going to surf. So, he took some painkillers, and we went on vacation with his daughter. It was his turn to spend two weeks in the summer with her. During the vacation, he was surfing, and after complaining about his pain, he would become excited and then anxious. He also began to display obsessive behavior. He would start talking about death, crying at night, checking the door several times before bed, and closing the windows to be sure no one could get in. Our room was on the fourth floor of an apartment block in a safe area, but still, he was obsessed with keeping the windows closed. He also began saying one thing one day and denying he said it the next. Additionally, he began making strange, repetitive movements with his hands, then holding my fingers and pressing on them regularly. I also noticed his daughter had some similar phobias and repetitive movements, particularly of her fingers. It was so weird for me.

I felt like I was going crazy in this reality. Francois kept insisting that everything was alright, but I knew it wasn't. It was clear to me at that point. It was a very difficult vacation. Later, Francois's mother asked me if I knew he had a manic depressive personality disorder. I replied that I did not know and asked her what it meant. She told me that he would need to tell me about it since he is supposed to take pills every spring and fall, but she also added that he doesn't do it. Needless to say, I was dumbfounded, but I was a loving wife-to-be, and I took it seriously. I would support him, and we would get through this struggle together. I proceeded to learn everything I could about the disorder and resolved that we would defeat it together. As it turned out, I was the only one in the struggle.

Soon, he began to criticize me—there's the devaluation tactic narcissists love to employ. For example, at the beginning of our relationship, Francois sent me a beautiful bouquet of roses. I had just gotten out of the shower, had no makeup on, and was dressed only in a red, silk robe when they arrived. I immediately took a picture of myself with the flowers and sent it to him. So, we were looking at this photo from early in our relationship with his mother only eight months later, and he remarked, "Wow, you look much older now." I asked how I could look so much older after only eight months. I knew I was still on top of my game as far as my appearance, and I was only 32 years old. I also knew I appeared offended, and he would tell me it was just a joke. That's yet another favorite tactic to make you think you're crazy. It was just a joke, yet it doesn't feel like that. It feels simply like a nasty insult. The goal is to distort your reality and make you think you're the one who's just being too sensitive; all the while, the psychopathic narcissist is insidiously stripping away your self-esteem. At this point in our relationship, the remark seemed so out of character for him, but this kind of thing began to happen more frequently until I realized it was *exactly* his character.

As his behavior started to change, I began tolerating these kinds of remarks regularly. I guess I was so caught up in what was beautiful about our relationship that I just couldn't face the reality of what was happening to it. I began changing my behavior to avoid his criticism. For example, he had to get up early to commute to work, which was 30 kilometers from Paris. With the traffic, it took him about an hour to get to work. On one occasion, he got up at 6 a.m. and was being really noisy as he took his shower.

I asked him kindly, "My love, could you please try to make less noise, as I'm sleeping?"

He yelled at me, "I'm the only person who works in this family. I wake up early to earn money for us, and you're asking me to be less noisy?"

After that, I understood that he was envious of my sleeping, so from then on, I decided to wake up early with him and go back to bed after he left if I needed more sleep.

As another example, he didn't sleep well. He usually took some pills to help him sleep, and even then, his sleep was very shallow and anxious. He needed to have the door and all the windows closed. For me, it was very suffocating, but if I opened the windows to have some air circulating in the room, he would blame me for his bad night's sleep. Thus, I tolerated it and suffered with no air circulation. I was also becoming more tolerant of his angry outbursts, always trying to adjust my own behavior to suit him.

His behavior was getting more and more obnoxious, however. He wouldn't let me wear any of my beautiful dresses that I brought to Paris. He said it wasn't typical for women in France to dress like that, but I knew he was worried I would outshine him. He wanted me to underline his greatness—not distract from it. I kept trying to remind myself of his good qualities, but by this time, I wasn't sure he had any. Still, I pressed on with the wedding plans. I felt as though I had come too far to turn back.

After our "family vacation," I needed a little time to rest and prepare myself for the most important event in my life. So, I went back to Ukraine to make the preparations and take my wedding dress. Our wedding would take place on a boat in Paris, and my entire family—my mother and my aunts—and my closest friends were all invited. They had already bought their tickets. What's more, my friends had prepared a Ukrainian dance in traditional costumes. I wanted everything to be perfect, so, although Francois paid for everything, I organized it all. I even planned to surprise our guests with appetizers of traditional Ukrainian cuisine.

I had begun to have doubts about the wedding. Everything was outwardly perfect. My dress was beautiful, and so was I, but I didn't have a good feeling. I wasn't sure I could handle Francois's secret mental disorder. My intuition was telling me to stay in Ukraine and just not show at the wedding. But I couldn't do that to my friends and family. They all had their tickets and were waiting for this day. I couldn't let them down. I am optimistic by nature, so I downplayed my fears. I told myself that everything would be great, and I was just experiencing the normal "cold feet." When I boarded the plane to return to Paris, I was upgraded to business class. I took that as a sign from the universe. Surely, I was just stressed because of the rapid changes I was experiencing in my life. I had a glass of champagne to relax as I flew into my new life.

The Big Day

My wedding was beautiful and what every girl would dream. Of the weddings I had attended, mine was by far the best. We were on a big boat on the Seine, the sunset was phenomenal, there was lounge music, my loved ones were all in attendance, and of course, I had my French love. It was my dream day. I had met my loved ones at the airport a few days earlier, so we could take a few days to see the sights around Paris. I had never imagined living in an overpopulated city with all the noise and traffic, but I had come to love this beautiful place. Now, I had the chance to rediscover it with my friends and family.

I was responsible for organizing every detail of our wedding: the music, photoshoot, decorations, my dress, my mother's dress, entertainment, and transportation—everything. I'm sure you can imagine how stressful this time was, but I wanted it to be perfect. I wanted to look beautiful that day, so I was naturally preoccupied with my hairstyle, dress, and makeup. It was a huge undertaking, and added to that was having to deal with my immature husband-to-be. Once again, I had a baby on my hands who was threatening a temper tantrum and complaining nonstop.

He was worried because many of his aristocratic relatives and friends were meeting me for the first time. To them, I was a simple girl from Ukraine, and they were very curious to know what I was like. We were doing a one-hour photoshoot near the Eiffel Tower before going to the boat where our friends and family were waiting. The photoshoot went great, but I could tell that Francois's anxiety was building. I needed all of my patience to calm him down. He was only concerned with his own feelings and needs. My back and feet were aching, but I had to hold perfectly still with a straight back, smile, and be friendly, even though I was exhausted and in pain. I was also hungry and stressed since I was representing Ukraine to his family and friends.

I wanted them to see that Ukrainian people are nice, intelligent, sophisticated, and down-to-earth, all at the same time. I was also worried that my French wasn't good enough, since I was still learning. I wanted Francois to be proud of his wife, but he had no concern for any of this since he was focused solely on himself. As we sat at a Parisian cafe waiting for a taxi, I finally asked him to please calm down. I told him I just couldn't stand it anymore. I was fed up with his egotism and anxiety. He seemed to think that I didn't need any support, as if I wasn't human. Everything was about him. I wanted to support him on this important day, but I also expected that he would support me. We were both in this together, after all. I decided to try a little psychology.

"My love, it's your party, and you are the host; people came here for you. So, be the king of this party, the big boss, and enjoy it because you are a superstar! It's your day and your shining hour! Let's rock it." I told him.

It seemed I knew almost intuitively what to say to a narcissist. I thought if he could calm down, we could both enjoy the day. When we arrived at the boat, we saw it was beautifully decorated and had about 60 guests onboard. He held my hand as we entered the corridor, filled with mostly French people. Francois was greeting his friends, so he let my hand go. I thought he should accompany his queen all the way in, but he was now starting to enjoy his party. I was just there to complement him. It wasn't a great moment for me, but I tried not to pay attention to my feelings at that time. I wanted everyone to enjoy themselves.

In front of our guests, he promised to love me, protect me, and do everything in his power to make me happy. We laughed, danced, and finally had fun. His friends were interested in my education and my work, and they were surprised that a simple girl from Ukraine had a good education, was intelligent, had nice manners, spoke five languages, and had her own business. They found me to be an appropriate trophy wife.

All of my friends and family were toasting our happiness and expressing their hope that we would have many children. They did the Ukrainian dance, treated the French guests to vodka and salo, the latter of which is a traditional type of Ukrainian bacon. They also gave us nice gifts. The French guests didn't give any toasts and brought fewer presents. In fact, my ten Ukrainian guests gave us as much as the 50 French aristocrats who attended our wedding. My husband was shocked by their miserliness and the generosity of the Ukrainians. The difference in mentalities was obvious for both of us.

My husband was fully in his element now. He was the king of his party. He was smiling, dancing, and enjoying himself. I noticed him flirting with some of our gay friends. He was, in fact, very obvious about it. I later learned that narcissists often have non-traditional sexual preferences, but at that time, I was just happy he was finally having fun. He was swimming in attention. That allowed me to have fun as well. It was everything I had ever dreamed of for my weddings. Dreams do come true, you know?

In the days following our wedding, we were in a euphoric state. My loved ones returned to Ukraine, and we began to live our normal life. We were going on our honeymoon in two weeks to Maldives. Francois just kept saying that after that, our real life would start. I still didn't know what he meant by that. Unfortunately, I would find out soon enough.

Signs You Married a Narcissist

It's not at all uncommon for people who have married a narcissist to say there was something magical when they first met. They often describe it as an irresistible pull toward someone who seems to match all of their needs and wants perfectly. It's equally as common for them to discuss how the fairy tale came to an abrupt end after they walked down the aisle. And, like I did, they often blame themselves for the problems that seem to erupt in their marriage overnight. Of course, it doesn't help that their narcissistic partner is telling them it's their fault. In fact, that's one of the signs you are in love with a narcissist. Let's take a look.

- **Blaming, Projecting, and Passing Out Free Guilt Trips**: Narcissists project their negative traits onto their spouse. It's not uncommon for them to tell you that you're needy, never satisfied, ungrateful, unapologetic, selfish, and have unreasonable expectations. These are all the same characteristics a narcissist has, but they project them onto you, so they don't have to deal with reality. They are also happy to blame you for any problem that arises. They might even belittle you in front of others and have a tendency to take minor events and blow them up into major arguments. They like to make themselves look superior by trying to make you look stupid or unreasonable.

- **Unreasonable Expectations**: Your narcissistic spouse expects you to meet their needs at all times. You're expected to anticipate how, when, what, and where the narcissist needs your admiration and adoration. It's also a one-way street because they take but never give it back in return. Moreover, no matter how much you give, it's never enough. You simply will be unable to satisfy their needs.

- **Jealousy**: The jealousy of a narcissist goes beyond the attraction of another person. They can be jealous of anyone or anything that captures your attention. That includes children, pets, friends, family, and work. They'll often go out of their way to demand your attention while you're on the phone, working on a project, talking to someone else, or engaging in an activity that requires your attention. Furthermore, their jealousy can trigger intense rage and even violence, something for which you will be blamed in the end.

- **Abusive Cycle**: Narcissists often provoke their spouse by being extremely cruel and/or abusive during an argument. They are setting the stage for their spouse to abandon them, and when that happens, they can then claim they were the victim of your abandonment. If you don't leave, they will gain more ammunition to use against you by provoking a response from you with their cruelty. They also don't take any responsibility for being so provocative. They see it all as your fault.

- **Abusive Behavior**: Narcissists punish their spouses by abusing or neglecting them. This can take the form of physical, emotional, financial, sexual, spiritual, verbal, or mental abuse. They might hit their spouse, send them on a guilt trip, withhold money, coerce sexual favors, use God to justify their behavior, intimidate, or gaslight them. They could also withhold love, attention, support, and communication as a form of mental and emotional abuse. They use various forms of manipulation in the sad attempt to get their needs met, needs that will never be satisfied. For a narcissist, there's nothing unconditional about their love. It is definitely performance driven.

- **Threatening Behavior**: Another tool in the narcissist's toolbox is to threaten abandonment, exposure, or rejection if their spouse doesn't comply with what they want them to do. The narcissist is an expert at identifying areas of insecurity in their spouse and using these to pressure them into doing what they want. In fact, in most cases, the narcissist identified this in their spouse before they proposed marriage. They are using their spouse's fears to keep them in the relationship longer. In addition, when a narcissist feels entitled to something, they use this tactic to get it, like a small child throwing a temper tantrum.

- **False Remorse**: Genuine remorse is something that takes time to implement before trust is reestablished. The narcissist, however, uses remorse to attempt to reestablish trust immediately. This is an unrealistic expectation. Additionally, if that doesn't happen and their spouse mentions the past behavior, the narcissist will become enraged. They will claim their spouse is unforgiving and use their lack of trust to justify repeating the offensive behavior.

These are all the warning signs that can indicate that you've married a narcissist. I was just beginning to see these characteristics in Francois. He was definitely prone to blaming me for things, had unrealistic expectations, got jealous if he believed I was taking attention away from him and had begun to engage in emotionally abusive behavior. This wouldn't be the end of it, either. I was about to see just how quickly the honeymoon would be over. Francois was just a narcissistic wolf in sheep's clothing, and he was about to reveal his true self.

Chapter Four: When the Honeymoon's Over—The Toxic Wolf Revealed

On the morning our honeymoon started, Francois had a conversation with his ex-wife. They had been talking about their daughter's phobia, which was getting worse. She had become a germaphobe, and her hands were now covered with wounds because she was overusing hand sanitizer. I think that somewhere deep down, Francois understood his own mental disorder and realized that was why his daughter also has a problem. However, since he was a narcissist, he couldn't stand to be blamed for anything; it made him angry. Needless to say, this conversation set the tone for our trip.

Honeymoon from Hell

At the airport, Francois was crazy. His mood was changing every five minutes. He vacillated between euphoria and aggression every few minutes. He must have gone from one to the other ten times while we were at the airport. It was so bad, and I was tired of trying to calm him down. This set the stage for our first big fight.

Francois decided I was flirting with an old man with whom I was talking about our honeymoon. I was telling him about where we were going and how great it was going to be, but Francois was jealous. Of course, jealousy is just another control technique. If you fall for that trap, they will soon have you averting your eyes and ceasing any communication with other men. Sometimes, a narcissist will even be jealous of your friends. For my part, I just couldn't stand it anymore, so I asked him to leave me alone. We didn't talk at all on the plane. I decided I wasn't going to dignify his behavior by paying any attention to it. I was not going to be swayed by his manipulative behavior. I wanted to show him that I didn't care, so I left him alone with his ego while I talked to an Australian woman returning from Paris.

After about an hour without me, Francois finally came looking for me. When he saw me talking in a friendly manner with another woman, he became very upset. He came up to me and whispered something bad in my ear. I don't remember the exact words he used, but they were designed to make me feel guilty for having left him alone with his bad mood. It wasn't surprising. I was becoming used to the idea that he didn't think I had the right to enjoy myself in any way if he was upset or couldn't enjoy himself too.

This time, however, I decided that I would treat him as he deserved to be treated. I simply wasn't going to care. This didn't sit well with him since he expected that I would be sad, guilty, and suffering, given his displeasure. I was supposed to be submissive and destroyed by his bad mood. He seemed to envy my inherent optimism and happy attitude. The truth is that I did feel terrible inside, but I wasn't going to show him. I put on a positive mask to indicate that I didn't care about him or his psychopathic mood changes.

We had a stopover in Dubai and decided to get some beach shoes for me since he had forgotten to pick up my summer footwear from his mother's house. I had been flying with sneakers on, but they wouldn't be good for the beach.

So, when we got off the plane, I said to him as if there wasn't any problem, "My Love, are you going with me to choose the sandals, or will you give me money to buy them by myself?"

He replied, "Why should I give you money?"

I answered, "Maybe because I'm your wife, and I don't have any sandals since you forgot to bring them from your mom's place?"

"I'm not going to give you any money. You can go back to Ukraine," he retorted with an angry, blaming tone of voice.

I replied, "I would go to Ukraine with pleasure, but I don't have a ticket at the moment, so we'll go together to Maldives."

I walked away from him and spent the next few hours walking alone through the airport, lonely, upset, and desperate. I couldn't even buy a bottle of water. He had left me without money, water, and sandals on the way to our honeymoon! This was the first time I considered divorce. At that point, we had only been married a couple of weeks. I can't begin to describe how distressed I felt. I was certain that a man who truly loved me would never make me suffer like that. No matter the circumstances, we are all humans. I couldn't imagine how things would be in the future if he was treating me like this now. My fairy tale romance was definitely over.

Paradise Lost

The person I loved and whom I thought was that special one had left me abandoned in the airport with no money. I just couldn't fit it into my picture of the person I had thought he was; he was being so cruel. Despite this, I wouldn't allow myself to cry. I put on a mask of indifference as I took a seat next to him on the next plane to Maldives. Neither of us spoke for the rest of the trip. I was being punished for being a bad wife, and he just felt I had to get used to it. I was fine until I saw the beautiful little islands of Maldives out the window of the plane. I couldn't help it; I started to sob.

I couldn't believe I was on the honeymoon of my dreams, but my dream was broken. His anger and craziness was not part of my dream. I had gotten what I thought was the man of my dreams, but my dream was quickly turning into a nightmare. I simply couldn't stop my tears. I had no mask anymore—only sunglasses to cover my eyes. Maybe he was touched by my tears or just ashamed to land in Maldives with his wife sobbing beyond control, but he tried to make up with me with a little love bombing. It didn't work. We argued the entire time at passport control. He would treat me nicely in front of other people, but whisper something terrible in my ear.

"Such hypocrisy, my Dear," I said as we were filling out the papers for check-in on the reception hall.

"Fuck you!" he shouted for everyone to hear and threw the papers in my face. Everyone in the reception area stopped drinking their cocktails to stare at us. No one had ever treated me like that before. I was shocked and angry. I thought of him as a psychopath. He wasn't even thinking about how we would be back here later, as we were on the same small island. He must have realized that, however, as he returned within five minutes to tell me he wanted a divorce. I said calmly that it was fine with me, but deep inside, I was just waiting to get to our bungalow where I could lay on the floor in the bathroom and cry. My pain was enormous. My dream was crumbling before my very eyes. I felt like a wounded animal with pain that was just killing me from the inside. I didn't care about him or what was going to happen next. I just wanted to be alone to cry, and then sleep and never wake up.

When we arrived at the bungalow, I silently passed by the beautifully decorated bed that said, "Happy Honeymoon." I smiled at what seemed like a joke now and closed the bathroom door behind me. I guess he must have worried that he had pushed it too far. He was afraid I would abandon him because the next minute, he was hugging me with tears in his eyes and begging me not to leave him (more love bombing). We both calmed down, and within one day, our relationship was back to normal, as if nothing had ever happened.

Real Life

After our honeymoon, I seriously began to question if I had made the right choice in a man. I saw everything as a trap. I was walking on eggshells. I had to be so careful because even though he seemed reliable and genuine, he had shown a peek at his real self. He had been so sweet in the beginning, and now it was so bitter. Just like he promised, real-life had started. Now, he didn't hold back. If something was irritating him, he started shouting. He blamed me for everything, including his bad mood. One moment, he hated me and was shouting at me, and the next moment, I was his lovely wife. It was madness.

Still, in the midst of all this, we were planning to have kids and looking for a bigger apartment to buy. He was promoted again at work, and as a result, his salary increased dramatically. He had, in fact, become one of the Vice Presidents of his corporation. After we met, his confidence had increased exponentially along with his sense of self-worth. I was helping along the way. I advised him on how to speak to his boss. I was definitely helping him. Francois was certainly an intelligent and charismatic man, but his career took off after we got together, all because his ego was growing larger by the day.

The most difficult times for me were on the weekends. For him, they were normal, but for me, they seemed like insanity. Anything that made him the least bit angry resulted in a fit of shouting. We had his daughter every other weekend. I felt particularly bad for her. She was really nice, but she had a number of phobias. She really couldn't enjoy her life because of her obsessions and anxiety. She took after her father. He didn't help matters either. When he tried to help her with her homework, it usually devolved into shouting and insults.

I remember him yelling at her, "Is that so hard to understand? Why should I have to repeat it to you more than once? Are you all right? You are completely stupid!"

She replied, "Daddy, please calm down. Please, don't shout."

I was in the other room just sitting on the bed and crying for this poor girl. She wasn't my kid, but my heart was breaking for her. After putting her down, he would come into the room and kiss me as if nothing had happened. I guess he was looking for admiration of his parenting skills. He thought he was a great father for helping her do homework. I just saw him more and more as a psychopath. This is a technique that toxic people often employ, usually with ex-partners, but it can also happen with other people. They put you on a pedestal while demeaning someone else. They can have you so flummoxed that you're just grateful they're no longer putting you down, but I couldn't stand watching him degrade his child.

I asked him through tears, "Please stop shouting at her. I beg you."

But it was all to no avail. He never believed himself to be guilty of anything. The more this went on, the more paranoid I became. I was trying to anticipate any little thing that could set him off, but it was an impossible task. I could never anticipate some of the things that made him angry. For example, one time we were spending a weekend at his mother's countryside house. We were in our bedroom one evening at midnight. He wanted to watch TV, but I wanted to go to sleep. I asked if we could turn the TV off and go to sleep, and that set him off.

"Don't I have a right to watch TV on my weekend? Why do you spoil everything?" He said.

I must have forgotten that I am only allowed to sleep when he does. Of course, the next day, I received the silent treatment for my sin of wanting to go to bed at midnight. It was becoming normal for him to treat me like shit. From my perspective, the situation was quite frightening and isolating. I was in another country, all alone. I didn't have my own home and was losing my best friend—my man, my husband. It was like I was sleeping with the enemy, which was not how I would have ever imagined things would be with him. I was also adjusting my behavior to try to avoid his bad moods. I wasn't comfortable sleeping while he was awake, so now I would get up with him, prepare a simple breakfast, help his daughter get ready for school if she was with us, and then, after he had left, I would go back to sleep again. Having to adjust my behavior to avoid conflict was also not something I would have ever imagined in my fairy tale marriage.

The Demise of Our Marriage

Francois had his hip surgery coming up, and of course, he became very stressed by that. I used that to justify his emotional instability, but it was taking a toll. I was starting to feel bad about myself. My self-esteem was dropping. I felt dependent on him in every way. I didn't have a job, and without a French education, I would be unable to get a job in the near future. Of course, he reminded me constantly of my dependence on him. Allowing that was my mistake, but I had trusted him. I could never have imagined the sweet man I had fallen in love with would hold money over my head.

On one occasion, we had a big fight that resulted in yet another silent treatment for me. I thought to myself that at least he didn't physically abuse me. But emotional abuse can do just as much damage—the bruises are just on the inside instead of the outside. He had wanted to manipulate my emotions. After the fight, he couldn't sleep. He let me know by breathing deeply to show me his suffering. Then, to further demonstrate his restlessness, he went to the bathroom without closing the door, left the apartment, came back, tried to sleep on the sofa, left again, and smoked inside the apartment. All of this was designed to bother me, and it did. I understood he was letting me know what a terrible wife I was and how much I made him suffer. So, the fight was on. I don't remember all the details, but he blamed me for his lost sleep. I told him he was not a child. He shouldn't throw a temper tantrum like one. I also told him I would not tolerate this. I said I didn't mind if he wanted to sleep on the couch. That was fine by me.

That wasn't the reaction he wanted, and although I seemed indifferent on the outside, on the inside, I was lonely and disappointed. Over time, I noticed these tantrums were one way he released his inner tension. He would use aggression, abusive behavior, and yelling to release his feelings, after which he would calm down and become the nicest man. It's an abusive cycle known as "hearts and flowers." One minute, he's treating me like a queen, then the tension builds, then an explosion, then regret, then back to being treated like a queen. It was a cycle of love-bombing followed by devaluation. I remember him telling me the story of his romance with a French woman. She was also a narcissist. He felt very stressed, manipulated, and frustrated by her behavior. In fact, he sought psychotherapy for it, and the therapist advised him to run away. I felt sorry for him when he told me the story, but now, ironically, I knew exactly how he felt.

Life had become a lunatic asylum for me. On one occasion, he, his daughter, his mother, and I all went to look at an apartment. On the ride there, he got a call from work. Something bad had happened in the factory, and he began yelling at his employee on the phone. We were all obliged to listen to this grown man act like a petulant child. He kept shouting the same things over and over again at his employee. I felt embarrassed for him in front of his mother and daughter, but it became clear they were accustomed to this kind of behavior from him. I seemed to be the only one who thought it wasn't normal, and that made me quite sad. I tried talking to him about it, but he would say things like that he was French and passionate, and it was normal for him. I even asked him to see a doctor, but he assured me he was completely normal and that I needed to adjust to the French culture.

Over time, I felt like I was losing myself. I stopped being the happy-go-lucky girl I had been before. I didn't smile as much nor allow myself the positive emotions I had always had in the past. I was becoming ever more anxious. I constantly felt a knot in my stomach. It's how I found out how anxiety feels. I had never felt like this before. It was like some kind of animalistic fear. The only time I was free of it was when I was sleeping. It was like a disease that was destroying me slowly from the inside out. I was apathetic and only wanted to sleep. I thought maybe my friend, who is a psychoanalyst, could help me. I had bought into Francois's claim that I needed to adapt to my new country. I thought maybe that explained the depression I felt.

I researched it, and the first two years you spend in another country when you're an immigrant can be very challenging. However, before I had the chance to do anything about how I was feeling, things got worse.

It was just before my birthday. We went to spend a weekend at Bretagne, in a five star spa and hotel, which was a wedding gift from his friends. I took my best heels and dresses, but when I put them on, Francois asked why I was wearing heels. He told me I looked taller than him. He had never complained about this before, and deep down, I knew he was concerned I would outshine him. I started to sense his envy quite often now. Every time I would share good news with him, he didn't seem happy about it. He was also envious of my appearance, youth, friends, family, kindness, optimism, and authenticity. It was as if my happiness triggered his sadness. I couldn't understand it.

It slowly became clear to me that Francois was afraid I could and would leave him. He had a desire to control everything. He even wanted to know exactly how much money I had in my Ukrainian bank account. He was using my dependence on him financially to try and keep me under control. He always nagged me about spending too much money on expensive food. As I realized that his own insecurity was at the root of this behavior, it became clear to me why he would treat me so cruelly, and he could be extraordinarily cruel. He knew my old wounds and sacred secrets. I had trusted him when I told him about them, and now he used them to hurt and attack me where I was weakest to show me once again that I was living with my enemy.

So it was that, at Bretagne, we had a serious fight. I had a feeling he wanted to spoil my birthday celebration. I was feeling so lonely in France, and the fact that I didn't have a loving, supportive home just made it worse. For my birthday celebration, his mother and daughter were going with us to a restaurant. I was getting dressed up, but he asked why I wanted to wear a dress. He told me I should just wear jeans. It felt to me like he didn't consider my birthday to be a cause for celebration, thus no need to get dressed up. At the dinner, no one wished me a happy birthday or said any nice words. It was just a typical dinner. His mother asked why I needed to order cake and wine with dinner, and she said we could have it at home.

When we got home, there was a cake from the supermarket waiting for me. It was beautiful and decorated with the number 33. That was the first time in my life I had a birthday cake with numbers on it, so for me it was special. We started to discuss cakes from Ukraine, and I offered to bake my favorite kind of cake for his birthday. I showed them all a picture of that kind of cake, to which my husband remarked, "Do you really eat that? It looks so terrible." More devaluation from someone who was supposed to love me.

"Daddy, you haven't even tasted it," his daughter said, taking my side.

Fighting back tears, I responded, "No worries, My Love. I will buy you a cake from the supermarket too. Less effort for me."

I wasn't crying because of the cake, I was crying because of his cruelty. His mother asked why I was so sensitive, to which I asked if that was a bad thing. They replied that they were just joking and asked if I didn't understand jokes. In truth, I was too sensitive for them, but I didn't want to show that. I was fighting back my tears, trying to numb myself while around them. I had a plane ticket to return to Ukraine in two days for a visit, and I was counting the hours to be back home with people who love me. I wanted so badly to escape the nightmare I was living in.

Saving Myself

For a second, I saw my future—*it was sad, depressing, and filled with anxiety*. I could see myself with a baby in my hands, exhausted and hopeless, without even the energy to smile. We would be living in a big Parisian apartment and the loan would be in my name as well as his. I could never afford the payments with no job, support, hope, or happiness. I slept with my enemy—one who puts me down and shouts at me all the time. I was scared and needy. *I was too sensitive.* I couldn't see a bright future or exit in this nightmare. I couldn't leave my baby and go back to Ukraine; I would never see my kid again. My husband had all the power. He had the job, money, and it was his country. He could kick me out on the street, and I would have no place to go. I would be one of the hundreds of homeless people I see in beautiful Paris. My optimism, inner joy, and beauty were all gone. When I looked in the mirror, I saw a desperate woman looking back at me, a victim. It was not at all what I had dreamt. I feel the anxiety of this vision in my stomach. It's living inside of me, toxically destroying me from the inside. What could I do? The only answer I could think of in that moment was to die. That's what jolted me awake. I had never had such thoughts before in my life. I love my life and wanted to live. The problem was that I didn't know how at that time.

When I arrived in Ukraine, my friends didn't recognize me. I was depressed and skinny. I had lost two kilograms after only one month of my happy marriage. I was so sad. I just wasn't myself. I felt lost, insecure, and stupid. It seemed that I didn't know what to do with my life. It was like I was in a fog. My fairy tale was gone, and I was left face-to-face with an ugly reality. I didn't have a man who could support or love me, and I didn't feel safe with him. I couldn't trust him to be there for me. He didn't make me feel beautiful or desired. With him, I felt old, awkward, and too sensitive.

I was visiting my mother for two days during my stay in Ukraine. While there, I got the idea to post on the Facebook group looking for advice from some Russian speaking women who lived in France. I told them that I was feeling like I just couldn't adapt to life there. I didn't have support from my husband, and he seemed to be putting me down and treating me like I wasn't even human. I never expected the answer I got from these women. They told me to run away immediately. They gave me all kinds of information about psychopaths, toxic people, and narcissists. Now, I'm grateful to them for opening my eyes.

That night, I spent half the night googling about some of these issues. I was discovering things about my husband from a different perspective. I discovered that what I had thought was true love was only love I had created in my head. What he felt was not about love. I discovered that he was a dangerous mix of psychopath and narcissist. His obsessions, pleasure in discussing the life of poor people, and many other cruel and strange things all pointed to his mental disorder. This was what I needed to see to wake up. I wondered how I got into this, but I realized I needed this experience. I didn't tell him what I found out. Instead, I continued to play the role of a calm and obedient wife.

Our communication while I was in Ukraine was very tense. I had to beg him for some money so I could spend the two weeks there. He sent me one hundred Euros. In the meantime, he was checking out another apartment with his mother and daughter. It was beautiful and in an old building that was just in front of the forest, but it was far from the supermarket and metro. He loved it, and it was a perfect match for his personality. However, it was not good for me or his daughter. We didn't have our own transportation, and it would make it hard for us to get out for school and shopping, particularly when it was cold and raining, which was quite often in Paris. He didn't care about that. He was concerned about his own status and the beauty of the place. He didn't think about comfort or convenience, and particularly not for us. He just wanted people to envy his life. He wanted that apartment so bad that he almost signed a pre-purchase agreement without me even seeing it. It was clear he didn't care what I thought. I was simply another possession in his life that he wanted people to be envious of, and as such, my opinion was not relevant.

When I told him that I would need to see the apartment before agreeing to buy half of it, his aggression kicked in. He called me ungrateful, silly, and said that I didn't understand the Parisian housing market. He also told me that it's not me who gets to decide. As his wife, I was supposed to just go along with what he wanted. When I didn't agree with him, he became irate.

He told me things like, *"You crossed a red line with your husband. I will put you down. You don't understand the reality of what you've done, but you will!"*

It was so vicious and frightening. I couldn't imagine someone who loves me speaking to me that way, but it just helped me understand that my suspicions were correct. He was definitely a psychopath.

I had only a few days before I was supposed to return to Paris. Every fiber of my being was telling me not to go back. I kept thinking that yes, I made a mistake, but it's not too late to escape. It was unbearable to live with the fear and anxiety I was experiencing. I spoke to my friend Lora who had also been in a relationship with a psychopath. She too had become very depressed, and now, I understood why. She recommended a book on psychopaths and narcissists for me to read. I read it and I started to make my escape plan. I had made the decision to seek a divorce in one night.

Although I knew I wanted a divorce, I had one huge disadvantage that brought me back to Paris. I am an empath, and as such, I have human feelings, a good upbringing, and a big heart. It's hard for me to leave someone in trouble if I can help. It's the rescuer that lives inside of me. Francois was supposed to have his hip surgery, and he would be unable to move for two weeks. He would need my help and support, and I couldn't leave him without anyone to help. I decided I had to support him during that time, but after that, I would leave. I just had to survive for 21 days. I bought a ticket back to Ukraine and brought plastic bags to pack my clothes for my return. I prepared myself mentally to play the role of a happy wife. Then, on Monday, December 3, when he returned to work after his surgery, I would disappear from his life with a one-way ticket.

I had to make sure Francois didn't sense my plan. He could be unpredictable, and I wasn't sure what to expect when he learned I was leaving. He could try to hit me, and since I'm an immigrant and he's a French citizen, even if I called the police, they might take his side. So, I prepared myself like I was going into battle. During my return flight to Paris, I read a whole book about toxic people and how to deal with them. By the time my plane landed in Paris, I was ready for the coming battle. I knew who he was in reality. I had a plan. I would pretend like nothing happened, even though we had problems over the past few weeks. I ignored the anxiety living inside of me. I knew that when I got away from this nightmare, I could take the time to heal myself. But, until then, I needed to stay calm. I needed to get through this to the day I could escape. I had told both my mom and psychoanalyst about my plan. My mom supported me after I told her what was going on. My psychoanalyst thought my husband and I were just having communication problems we could work out, the same thought some of my friends. But I knew differently. If you never faced it, it's hard to understand what is emotional abuse. I was listening to my heart now, and it was saying, "Run away!" That was exactly what I was going to do.

Universe, please *help me*!

Leaving a Narcissist

My worries were justified. It's not easy to leave a narcissist. In fact, it's likely to be one of the hardest things you'll have to do in your life. Narcissists depend on the people in their lives for their own supply of self-esteem. They need someone they can abuse and manipulate to fulfill their need to feel better, stronger, and smarter than anyone else in their lives. Additionally, after the emotional rollercoaster, I had been on—the sudden mood changes from extreme highs to harsh and often aggressive lows—I was exhausted, which is not uncommon. To put having to uproot my life on top of the emotional trauma I had already suffered was almost too much to bear.

The things you have to remember if you're going through a similar trial are all the reasons that caused you to decide to leave in the first place. You need to keep trusting your gut and set firm boundaries to stick to your plan. It is also true that you are in a potentially dangerous situation, so you have to take care as you go through this process. The following are tips for getting out in the safest way possible.

No More Chances

It takes on average seven times before most people will get out of an abusive relationship. Perhaps you do get out and they will try to seduce you back, just so they can be the one to dump you. Everything needs to be on their terms, and if they're physically violent, they will usually become even more abusive. If they aren't violent with you, they may try to plead with you to stay and tell you how sorry they are, but regardless of what strategy they use to try to win you back, it's important that you don't give them another chance to hurt you again. Narcissism is a disorder that requires years of therapy to treat, and without a strong commitment from the afflicted person—something that's difficult to get since most narcissists believe the problem is with everyone else—treatment is not likely. Giving them one more chance will just result in more pain for you and the loss of your precious time.

Don't Tell Them You're Leaving

My instinct not to tell Francois I was leaving was the right thing to do, according to experts. One of two things will happen if you do: they will love bomb you to try to keep you from leaving, or their behavior will become even more aggressive and potentially dangerous. They may increase their angry outbursts, threaten you physically, or even threaten something you cherish, such as your children, pets, or keeping some of your items. That's why it's better to make a plan to get out and just leave. If you have to talk to them, do it from the safety of your new home, then try to avoid in-person discussions or confrontations.

Make and Keep Copies of All Your Documents

Remember that a narcissist needs you to fulfill the needs created by their illness. That means they will do everything in their power to keep you from leaving, which could mean hiding important, identifying documents like your passport or residency documents if you're from another country. That was my situation in France, and I did keep my own documents. I was lucky that was something I did because it was my personality. I would have trusted Francois in the beginning, so it wasn't because of any special insight on my part; it was just my habit. In some cases, a narcissistic abuser might not let you keep your own documents. In that case, you might need to trick them to get the documents and make copies or hide them away where only you can find them. You might, for example, tell them you need your documents to fill out an application. If you know where your documents are, you could simply wait until your abuser is out of the house to retrieve them.

Spare Cash

If you're thinking of leaving, you will want to tuck away some money, so you can have enough to cover your expenses until you get settled. I never would have thought Francois wouldn't share money with me when I needed, but that's what happened when I went home for a visit. He showed his true colors and tried so hard to control me. Depending on your circumstances, you might have to do this a little at a time, secretly, so your abuser won't cut you off altogether.

Talk to Someone

If your abuser is physically violent with you, it's important to report it to the police. You want to document what happened so there is a record of it. Even if your abuser is not physically violent, it's vital that you talk to someone about what is happening. First, it's not uncommon for victims of this type of abuse to become isolated from friends and family. That's intentional on the part of the abuser. They don't want you to have anyone who might help you leave them. That takes an emotional toll, and it's easy to believe that you are wrong or the crazy one. Having someone to talk to, whether it's a family member or even your doctor, can help you document what's happening, and you'll see that you're being abused and need to think carefully about your options.

Log Out

If you stay logged in to any of your abuser's devices, it would provide them with a way to track what you're doing. Before leaving, carefully make a list of any device you've logged into or entered credit card details into, as well as any sites where you have auto-fill turned on. Go through and delete all of these. If you use a program like LastPass to save your passwords, do a master reset to create a security boundary. If your abuser commonly takes things away from you, make sure you have a cheap burner phone. They last forever without recharging, and you'll have it if you need it.

Check for Trackers

It's not uncommon for abusers to put a tracker on your phone. One sign that indicates that it has happened is if your battery keeps draining. Another clue is if you have a Kindle and when you log in, it reminds you of the book that was the last read yesterday, though you can't remember reading it then. That could mean someone is tracking what you're reading. You'll also want to eliminate the history on your web browser, so your abuser can't see what you've been looking up online. You can also set your browser not to track your online history.

Don't Believe the Flattery

It often happens that a narcissist swings wildly between loving flattery and extreme anger. When they sense problems, they will often resort to extreme flattery to try to calm you down and keep you from leaving. They can make you feel like there's no reason to leave. Everything is fine, and in fact, it's become just what you want. The truth is, however, that this is only a temporary situation, and as you've already experienced—just like I did with Francois—the psychopath will return. You deserve better than this, just like I did. You deserve someone who won't play with your emotions, so even if things get temporarily better, don't believe the flattery.

Reconnect with Friends and Family

Narcissists like Francois actively try to cut you off from your friends and family. They don't want you to have anyone else to turn to; that makes them believe you'll stay with them. Toward that end, they may try spreading rumors and fear to isolate you from your loved ones, and they'll definitely try to keep you from connecting with them in person. You have to remember that your loved ones are on your side. Don't be embarrassed or afraid; just reach out to them. They'll help you understand your true worth and that you don't deserve the emotional and/or physical abuse you're enduring. They'll also be there for you when you decide to leave.

Cut Out Other Toxic Relationships

This is a good opportunity to take stock of your friends and eliminate any others who might also be toxic. Your true friends and loved ones will want nothing but the best for you. They won't blame you when things go wrong, nor will they abandon you. Those that do are not real friends, so get them out of your life. Take this time to surround yourself with true friends who will help you rebuild your life.

Stay Away after Leaving

Although it can be hard to leave your life behind, it's the best way to move on. You're losing your hopes and dreams, so it's definitely difficult to let go. It's also easy for your brain to remember the good times and forget the bad, but in the case of an abusive relationship, it's critical to remember the bad times. If you go back, the bad times will return, so remember that the narcissist is particularly good at hiding their true nature. That doesn't mean they've changed, just that they're hiding the ugliness from you.

Don't Fall for Sob Stories

Because of my empathic nature, this is particularly difficult for me, but even if you're not an empath, narcissists are experts at tugging at heartstrings. They'll tell you how sorry they are or that they need you for one reason or another. They might also show up unexpectedly on special occasions like your birthday. They'll tell you that they just couldn't stay away, or, like Francois, they'll write you a letter telling you how much they miss you, or that they just can't stop thinking about you. This is all manipulation. There's something called a "drama triangle," where a person would flip from being a savior to a persecutor to a victim. The narcissist does just this. They convince you how much you need them (savior), then they start abusing you (persecutor); then, if you threaten to leave, they will suddenly become the victim you're abandoning. The "drama triangle" is like the infamous Bermuda Triangle of relationships—it will make your self-esteem disappear, so don't fall for it.

Remember the Roller Coaster Ride

A relationship with a narcissist, as you can see in my story, is like a roller coaster ride; there are highs, lows, twists, and turns. There is no stability and little opportunity for a healthy relationship to develop and thrive. If you keep getting on the ride, the result will be the same. There's little chance for the outcome to be any different than it was before, so remember how frightening and unstable that ride feels and opt instead for a ferris wheel.

Get Rid of Gifts

It's just better overall to get rid of anything that reminds you of the narcissist. If you don't need it, give it away. That chapter of your life is in your past, so it's time to move on by ridding yourself of those painful reminders.

Ground Yourself

When you've been through a traumatic experience created by a relationship with a narcissist, you need to work that trauma out of your body. It can definitely cause post-traumatic stress disorder if it gets out of hand, and that is something you simply can't ignore. By learning to ground yourself in the present moment and sit with the emotions you're experiencing, allowing them to flow out of your body, you can then reclaim yourself and heal the trauma you've experienced. It can also help to understand what it was that attracted you to this person in the first place, so you can break out of any unhealthy patterns.

Gray Rock Method

Because it may not be possible for you to cut off contact altogether with your toxic partner—you might have children together, for example—it's good to know a strategy that can cause them to lose interest in you. One strategy is called the Gray Rock method. It's a great way to get rid of a persistent psychopath in your life. Because narcissistic psychopaths feed on drama, the idea behind this method is to starve them of any drama. The key is simply to give boring, monotonous responses to them whenever you come in contact with them. Eventually, your boring responses retrain their brain to expect boredom rather than drama in any interaction with you. In time, they'll find someone else to provide them with the drama they crave, and they will be drawn to you less frequently.

This method is a great way to get the psychopath to go away on their own, and it's also a helpful way to avoid becoming a target in the first place if you're being pursued by a narcissistic psychopath. Additionally, this method is useful if you have narcissists in other areas of your life. Perhaps you work with one or they are a member of your family. By portraying yourself as boring when with them, they will have no interest in interacting with you. Even if they do begin to target you, Gray Rock can still help you direct their attention elsewhere. The name Gray Rock gives you an image to focus on when you're in an emotionally charged situation. Simply imagine a gray rock, and do more than visualize it—become it! When you are the gray rock, your narcissistic abuser will lose interest and look for a more dramatic person.

Make a List

Write down the bad things you experienced in your relationship, so you have a solid reminder of why you needed to leave. Every time the narcissist contacts you, read that document, so you aren't fooled by the sweet things they might say. Those sweet nothings are just that: nothing, but they can still generate a flood of oxytocin to your brain that could make you feel kindly toward them. Having a list will help you remember that what they're saying isn't real. Although you might have empathy for your abuser, it's vital to also have empathy for yourself. Think about how you would feel if someone was treating your very best friend in the world that way. You would be livid, so why would you allow anyone to treat you that way? Be as kind to yourself as you would to your best friend.

These tips are all things to remember as you prepare to leave your abuser. They will help you have a much smoother transition from life with a narcissist. It is a leap of faith, but have faith because a new life is out there waiting for you—one in which you are valued and loved, and that's a leap of faith worth taking.

Chapter Five: A Leap of Faith— Divorcing a Narcissistic Husband

When I got off the plane to Paris, he met me with a bucket of flowers. He was looking deeply into my eyes, no doubt wondering what I planned to do. I could see he was not sure of my reaction and thinking that he may have been too hard on me. For the next few days before I arrived, we hadn't talked, since we were still arguing. He didn't realize it, of course, but I had already made the decision to seek a divorce. I didn't feel the need to speak to him anymore, but I tried to act like nothing was different when I arrived.

As we drove home, you would have thought we were a normal couple. I was tired and went to sleep after the flight. In reality, I was biding my time and counting the hours I would have to be with him before he needed to go to the clinic for his operation. I was careful to take birth control measures since that was a mistake I could not afford. That night, we had great sex. He was a great lover, and sex was always good with him. Still, I didn't know how I could enjoy it with him after my decision, though I adjusted so he wouldn't suspect anything. For him, sex was a way to confirm that everything was alright between us. So, I put my heart and soul aside and simply gave him my body as a present, a final gift before leaving him.

After sex, he calmed down, and within two days, he began to relax, since he believed everything was under control. That's what I wanted. I kept playing the part of a good wife and went to see the apartment he liked. On the last night before his operation, he once again wanted sex. I went to take a shower, as was my habit, and when I came out of the bathroom, he was pretending to be asleep. I thought that he must have been tired after a long day, and I was happy he was giving me a reason not to have sex with him. Still, I knew he was pretending to check my reaction. It was evident because he was overacting, snoring like he had never done before. He appeared to be soundly asleep, but my intuition knew better.

I decided to play the game too. I calmly fell asleep at his side. I soon woke to his temper tantrum, telling me what a terrible wife I was. I wouldn't be lucky enough to get sleep that night. He stormed around the apartment, shouting at and blaming me. He was telling me I was a stupid, bad wife, and that he didn't know how I couldn't understand that he wanted me to give him a blowjob. In his mind, I would be the sexy wife, waking my sleepy husband with a blowjob. But I was not in the mood to play these games. I couldn't read his mind, and I wasn't in the mood for his tantrum. He claimed that I was a terrible wife and that even his ex could "sense" when he needed a blowjob.

"Why did you marry me if I am so terrible?" I finally shouted.

He yelled in response, "You don't love me and don't want to have sex with me!"

I told him calmly that we were going to the clinic tomorrow and needed to get some sleep. My calm voice made him even more crazy. He once again told me that I was a bad wife who made him suffer. Little did he know that I wasn't really his wife anymore. I was just a spectator watching the show. That's why I could be so calm, which was just driving him crazy. By 2 AM, I was sitting in a chair with my silk slip on, watching him shouting. I always forgot that whenever he was overwhelmed with emotions, I didn't have a right to sleep or do anything until he was calm again. I waited for the tantrum to end, knowing that I wouldn't have to put up with it much longer. All I could think was that this show was getting boring, and I could be sleeping instead of doing this. It was more than enough.

I was grateful for his tantrum, though, since I felt it gave me the right to change the date of my ticket to return to Ukraine. I silently thanked the universe for this affirmation that my decision was the right one. It seemed unbearable to me to spend even one more day with this psychopathic man-child. The next morning, I told him that I was not going to tolerate his disrespect and hysterical displays anymore. I reminded him we had discussed this before, and now, I was simply fed up. I was calm while I told him that I would take him to the clinic, but after that, I would leave on the next possible flight to Ukraine. I told him that he had made my life in France terrible and I couldn't tolerate his attitude toward me anymore.

The next available flight was in four days. I sent my clothes home ahead of time and went to visit Francois in the clinic. He tried to melt my heart and change my mind. He was putting on a show of suffering and pain. He asked me weakly to hold his hand, and I forced myself to do it. I thought to myself that it was like playing a role in a movie. He told me how much he needed me in his life and that he loved me. He also said he hoped I had changed my mind. The way he spoke almost made him seem like he was dying. I replied that I was too bad of a wife for him, and it's better that I leave, playing his game a bit. I told him that he deserved someone better. I said all of that with inner joy at the knowledge that I was getting out.

I left the family ring that his mother had given me and all the clothes he bought for me. I also left that part of my life there. While I waited for my flight, I slept on the floor in my friends' rental room because I just couldn't stay at Francois's place anymore. I also visited my favorite places in Paris at this time and made sure to see the famous streets. It was difficult for me to say goodbye to the city I had come to love, but I promised myself I would think about all of that later. Right now, I had to follow my plan and get someplace safe. In a way, I was like a zombie. I didn't allow myself to feel; I just acted. I organized everything that I wanted to take and left the necessary documents for him to start divorce proceedings. I wrote down that I was leaving him because I could no longer tolerate his emotional abuse. I put my full name by the statement and signed and dated it. I also showed it to the police and told Francois about it. I can't tell you how grateful I am to all the people who supported me during these very difficult days.

For Francois's part, he couldn't believe I was serious. His mother even called me to ask if I would give him one more chance. I cried to her. I cried because my dreams and heart were broken, and I felt as if my soul had been destroyed. I cried for the lie that was our relationship, and I cried for the huge mistake I had made by marrying him. His mother acknowledged that he needed long-term psychotherapy but still insisted that it was no reason to get a divorce. I couldn't believe what she was saying; this man had made me think about suicide for the first time in my life, and if that wasn't a good reason for a divorce, what was?

On November 20, I landed in Ukraine. The day was rainy and gray, and as soon as I entered my home, I fell asleep. I had my real estate and some savings, so I had some time to recover from what had happened. I wasn't so naive that I hadn't protected myself some, just in case. I had enough money to not have to get a job for a year or more. That would give me time and resources for doing what I needed to do to recover. I was 33-years-old, so it wasn't too late to start a new chapter in my life, and it was definitely too early to give up. I wanted to recover and move on, but I also knew that would be a process in and of itself.

Initial Steps Toward Recovery

When you just leave your toxic partner, you will experience a myriad of emotions. It can be overwhelming, but a few tips can help you navigate the early stages of grief. The important thing to realize is that you're out now, and the healing can finally begin. Here are a few things to remember as you begin the journey to your recovery:

Allow Yourself to Grieve: It's normal to be sad after the loss of an intimate relationship. Just because you're happy to be free from the suffering doesn't mean you won't feel sadness at the loss. You will also be a bit disoriented at first, so it's a great idea to pamper yourself. Watch different kinds of movies, eat a pint of ice cream, cry to your family and friends, and let yourself feel your grief. It's truly the only way it will clear out of your system. You've just come out of a battle, so give yourself a little downtime and a lot of self-love.

Don't Doubt Your Decision: It's not uncommon after a breakup—even one with a toxic partner—to think you've made a mistake. Suddenly, you're out on your own, facing a lot of uncertainty. The devil you know can seem better than the unknown, but it's not. You made the right decision, because you chose the path that would lead you into genuinely healthy, happy relationships. Don't forget that that is your goal. You can reach it, but not if you go back.

Cultivate Self-Love: This is a time in your life when you're going to need all the self-love you can get. You've been made to doubt yourself and your abilities as a result of the narcissistic abuse you've suffered, so now it is time to remember all the great things about you. Fire your inner critic and replace those negative thoughts with positive affirmations. These have been shown to retrain your brain so positivity is your first response, no matter what setbacks you face. It's important to remember that the most important relationship you will ever have in your life is the one you have with yourself.

Unleash Your Creative Side: Paint, dance, write poetry or the next great American novel, take a cooking class, start a new project, learn to play a musical instrument, or learn a second language. Do something to unleash your creativity in a way that will allow you to express your feelings through a variety of different activities. It will give you something else to focus on other than your sadness. It will also help you clear the trauma from your body, mind, and soul.

Spend Time with Loved Ones: It's not uncommon for narcissists to make you cut ties with loved ones. This is a good time to reconnect with people who truly love you and want the best for you. It's important that they not be toxic people, but rather, people who genuinely have your best interest at heart. Being around people who really love you at this time can help you to banish any self-doubt and find your way forward.

Stay Present: The thing about the present moment is that you notice how everything is constantly changing, including your feelings. Initially, you might feel like you'll never get over the loss of not only your love, but your dreams of a wonderful marriage and that perfect family. However, if you sit in the present moment, you'll find that the feelings of sadness ebb and flow and are diminished with every passing day. You'll also allow yourself to sit with your feelings of grief, and that will help you let the feelings move through rather than get stuck inside of you. You might think you don't want to do that nor want to feel those depressing emotions again, but if you face them head-on, you'll find it will be easier to let them go. That will help you move on much faster than you could otherwise.

Remember Who You Are: It's easy to lose yourself in a relationship, particularly one that involves a narcissistic partner. Right after leaving, it's a good idea to get back in touch with the real you—the wonderful, positive person who lived inside you before you were ever traumatized by a wounded psychopath. To rediscover yourself, try taking up some of the hobbies you had before your relationship but gave up because your ex wasn't interested. Go back to your roots and let yourself remember the happy, carefree you that existed before your toxic relationship.

Chapter Six: The Traumatic Effects of Escaping a Toxic Relationship— After the Storm

The next day after arriving in Ukraine, I didn't want to wake up. I didn't see sense in my life anymore. I had lost my family, business, and dream. Every fiber of my being was screaming, "I don't want to wake up!" I could only hope I had imagined this, that maybe he wasn't the monster I thought he was. Maybe I had to work on myself. I could tell I was in for a rough ride. It was hard too. I vacillated between thinking on some days that everything had not been so bad, that maybe I was just being too sensitive. There were a lot of maybes on those days, but in my body, and with the level of anxiety I had felt, I just knew that I had made the right decision. I had decided to survive and give myself a better life.

All the while, he was texting me, blaming me for abandoning him, and telling me how much he loved me. He even accused me of causing his daughter trauma. According to him, I was the guilty one—guilty for everything that had gone wrong in his life. I had to keep telling myself that I loved me and wanted to be happy. It was an extremely difficult time in my life. I experienced serious depression that I needed to overcome. I knew I was experiencing a complex post-traumatic stress disorder (C-PTSD) as a result of what happened. It took me one full month for the initial recovery, and during that time, I let myself do whatever I wanted. I slept as long as I wanted, ate what I wanted, and did what I wanted.

After a month of allowing myself to get over the initial effects of the breakup, I had to start planning for the rest of my life. I let myself suffer during that month, so I could begin to heal my wounds. I ate junk food—chips, cakes, alcohol—and even smoked. I slept until noon and went to yoga two times per week. I was also reading about narcissists, and the more I read, the more confident I became in my decision to leave. I also started going on dates and even tried sex with one guy. It was important to begin the process of seeing myself with someone new.

I alternated between pampering myself and just wallowing in my sorrow. My friends supported me as much as they could, but some of them couldn't understand. If you've never had to endure this kind of treatment, it is difficult to understand why other people would put up with it. Well, it only takes one experience with it, and you'll never allow it again. Once you survive narcissistic emotional abuse, you know the smell of the enemy. Make no mistake about it—there were some evenings when I cried in the dark, but as the days passed, the pain became less and less.

Francois and I started the divorce proceedings. He even agreed to spousal support payments of 300 Euros for three months. He was nothing if not generous, and I mean that sarcastically. He was also texting me messages full of hate and anger, which caused me to sink back into depression, but more and more, I was able to recover from those momentary relapses. After about two weeks, he wanted to come and discuss our relationship, but he was constantly blaming me for being weak and unprepared for a real relationship. He wrote that I ran away as soon as our family life had started. I was not ready to see him, and I didn't think there was a need to meet with him in person. I was still anxious, and that was something that stayed with me for a few months. I tried yoga, meditation, and pills to relieve stress, but nothing seemed to help. It finally passed, but when I saw another narcissistic predator coming my way, it returned.

December passed, and I celebrated the new year with my mom. It was a cozy and calm atmosphere. After that, I decided to try taking some courses for a new job, and I went on vacation with my friend Lora. I also started dating more. Now that I could spot a narcissist even from photos and text messages, I knew I could avoid falling into that trap again. Six months after I escaped that relationship, I went to Paris for the divorce. Francois didn't say hello, goodbye, or anything really. It was like I was nothing to him. I told him I was grateful for the experience I gained from our relationship; then, I blocked him on all of my messaging apps.

It's been two years since my escape from that nightmare, and a lot of things have changed. I have read much literature about NPD, borderline personality disorder (BPD), and other disorders within cluster B. I have learned much about why they are that way and watched hundreds of videos on the subject. I know so much about narcissists and how they feel now. It has enabled me to recognize people displaying traits of NPD all around me. I even did a deep dive into my own childhood and was able to recognize how my own father may have suffered from this disorder. I have also had an opportunity to seek treatment for my C-PTSD that resulted from my experience.

Now that the storm has passed, I can be grateful for the lessons this experience brought me. I can also say that it helped me work on myself. I had made mistakes, ignored the warning signs, and wanted to understand why and work on the problem. My marriage helped me take a deeper dive into my own problems and discover more about myself, with the help of my psychoanalyst. We spent many hours discussing this, and I now understand that I had problems setting appropriate boundaries. I let my ex-husband cross those boundaries easily. I was afraid to be myself and express my emotions and what I wanted. I relied on someone else for my sense of self-esteem, and that fact made me very easy to manipulate.

It took time for me to heal myself and start a new life, but now I can spot when someone is trying to manipulate me, and I can turn that around. I also know this message is important for everyone to know—it doesn't matter if you're married or not; it's critical to have your own savings and a Plan B. By having a Plan B, you will have more than one way to go, and your life won't end in sadness. You will have a plan to ensure you can find your "happily ever after," even if it doesn't include a partner.

The greatest sign I had that I had recovered was when my anxiety finally went away. Even when Francois wrote me on Skype to request that I add him as a contact and that we start over again from scratch, I didn't feel anxious. I didn't feel any emotions—none as I ignored his message. That's when I knew I was finally better, and when I knew that, I realized how grateful I was for this important life lesson.

It's helpful to remember that every challenge we face is an opportunity for growth. When I looked at the hidden opportunities inside the challenging toxic marriage with Francois, I realized that I had my own issues of low self-esteem. This experience helped me strengthen my sense of self-worth and self-confidence. It taught me that I can survive anything and come out stronger than ever before. I now have a renewed confidence in myself, and I don't believe I will ever lose myself again in a toxic relationship.

One thing I should mention is that my story was luckily less complicated than most others because we did not have children together. For those stuck in these relationships with children, you'll have to be even more courageous in breaking the ties with your partner, and of course, unless you can show they are abusive to the children, they will likely remain a part of your life. However, this doesn't mean you should stay with them for the sake of the children. In fact, it's even more imperative that you get out of that environment, so your children will have a healthy refuge. In my second book on recovery from abusive relationships, I'll present some specific strategies for helping children survive a narcissistic parent.

Additionally, my situation did not involve physical abuse. Many involved with narcissistic psychopaths do experience physical abuse from their partner. This is an incredibly dangerous situation, and you must get yourself and any children you have out of it. As part of that process, you should record everything. If he harms you, take pictures and tell someone, preferably the police. However, if you don't feel secure calling the authorities, tell other people in your life and document everything he does. There are also often domestic violence support organizations in your country of residence. Seek those out and get yourself to safety. I'll have more to say about this in my next book on this subject, but you should never have to fear for your physical safety.

My story has a happy ending, and I want your story to have one too. If you find that you're in an emotionally abusive relationship, please know that I am sending you a hug. I am also advising you to start planning your escape. You deserve better than that just like I did. I hope my story can help you find a way out.

Final Words

Narcissistic Personality Disorder is a difficult mental disorder to deal with if you're living with someone who has it. The narcissist doesn't see that anything is their fault, yet it is their deep-seated insecurity that guides their manipulative, often aggressive, and always vanity-driven behavior. The ego of the narcissist is extremely fragile because in reality, they live with crippling insecurity. It's so bad, they have to tear other people down to boost themselves up. That's exactly what I experienced.

They are also experts at distorting reality. I felt like I was living in a funhouse where the mirrors make you look tall and skinny or stunted and fat. My reality was nauseatingly distorted, and I never knew what to expect from one minute to the next. It was truly a roller coaster ride. One minute he was love-bombing me, and the next he was insulting me. I could never please him. He always expected more of me, and gone was my loving husband who supported my dreams.

Often, people don't understand how you ever got to be with someone who treated you like that. They judge you for not acting soon enough, but what they don't understand is that the psychopathic narcissist wasn't always like that. In the beginning, they were charming, supportive, admiring, and loving. You think you've hit the jackpot with a loving partner, only to find that it was all a grand illusion. Hidden behind that mask of love was an ugly monster, a veritable Mr. Hyde.

It's a difficult life lesson, but one that brings many strengths as you pull yourself out of the abuse and rebuild your life. You see the inner strength you truly have and step up to give yourself the love you were hoping to find with your partner. That is what you must do for yourself. If you stay in your abusive relationship without a solid and loving sense of self, you will suffer irreparable and constant harm. You deserve better than this; everyone does. It's just that not everyone can give love. That's the problem, you see: the narcissist can't love. They don't know how. They have never been able to love themselves, and without self-love, you simply can't truly love someone else.

Of course, it's best to avoid these types of relationships altogether by learning to spot the warning signs, but narcissists are very good at hiding their condition. It's important to understand that it's not your fault if you didn't see the toxicity, and you should not feel ashamed for having fallen for their charming personality. However, when you realize the situation you're in, you need to take steps to rescue yourself. It's not uncommon for this kind of relationship to leave you with a complex post-traumatic stress disorder (C-PTSD), and that will stay with you unless you treat it by getting yourself out of the abusive situation and rebuilding your life.

If you're interested in knowing more about how to do that, please check out my Emotional Abuse Recovery Workbook on the subject. You see, one of the things that I learned from my experience is that I have a genuine desire to help others escape the nightmare of narcissistic abuse. Toward that end, I earned a degree in psychology and learned as much as I could about NPD and all the other personality disorder combinations.

I felt so alone when going through this experience. If this book can help you feel like you have someone in your corner, then I have made a difference. I want to help you recover from your abusive relationship and find the happiness you truly desire and deserve. You might think you made a mistake, just as I thought, but you do have a choice. You don't have to remain emotionally abused. There is a road to recovery from the trauma, and I want to show you the way with this book and my second book FREE YOURSELF, which will take you through a Complex PTSD recovery program from an emotionally abusive relationship. Please feel free to contact me anytime; I will be glad to be your narcissistic abuse recovery coach, and I will help you heal and start with a new, healthy relationship.

By sharing my experiences, I hope to help you realize that you are not alone or crazy, and there is hope. You can get out and recover. You've taken the first step by buying this book. My message to you is that you deserve a happy life filled with true love—don't settle for less than that.

I hope you've been helped by this book, and I truly would like to hear your feedback. Please take a moment to leave your review. Reviews on Amazon are incredibly helpful—both for other readers to decide whether the book will be useful to them and for new authors like myself to get the word out. So, your support is very important. I truly appreciate feedback from my readers, and I love to hear success stories. I hope to hear one from you soon!

Thank you!

Love yourself and be brave!

A wonderful life is waiting for you ahead!

Warm regards,

Elena Miro.

COMPLEX PTSD
RECOVERY WORKBOOK FOR WOMEN

FREE
YOURSELF

10 STEPS TO GO
FROM EMOTIONAL ABUSE RECOVERY
TO BUILDING HEALTHY RELATIONSHIPS

E L E N A   M I R O

FREE YOURSELF!

A Complex PTSD Recovery Workbook for Women

10 Steps to Go from Emotional Abuse Recovery to Building Healthy Relationships

Elena Miro

Introduction

My relationship started out great, but it didn't take long before he was treating me terribly. After the shock of realizing what was happening, I broke free, but the healing process took a while to accomplish. If you're in a toxic relationship and thinking about leaving or have already left your partner, this book is for you. I have put together this workbook to help you overcome the Complex PTSD that is typical after being involved in an emotionally abusive relationship.

The first thing you have to do is identify your situation. Are you in a relationship where your partner has started to treat you badly after at first treating you like a queen? Are you wondering if it's just temporary, or are you definitely in a toxic relationship? Do you think you're going a little bit crazy? Are you considering leaving him but aren't sure what to do? If any of this rings a bell, the first thing to know is that you're not alone. The second thing to know is that you're not imagining things. You don't deserve any of the poor treatment you were subjected to! The third thing to recognize is how the trauma from emotional abuse is taking its toll.

You might be surprised, but you don't have to be a combat veteran to suffer from C-PTSD. In fact, consistent emotional abuse—and even physical abuse—can leave you just as emotionally wounded as actual combat would. You might be suffering from symptoms like depression, anxiety, insomnia, and many others as a result of the unpredictable and denigrating treatment you received from being in a relationship with a narcissistic man.

You might also be wondering how you will ever get your life back together, and maybe even how you can possibly go on without him. All those feelings are valid, and they're exactly why I wanted to write this book: to help you heal from the trauma you have suffered. I've been there, and so have many other women. You can read my story in my first book, *My Toxic Husband: Loving and Breaking Up with a Narcissistic Man—Start Your Psychopath-free Life Now!* But this book is meant to help you heal. I not only lived through what you're going through now, but it inspired me to learn more about the condition. That's why I decided to get a degree in psychology and learn as much as I could about the relationship that left me questioning myself, doubting my abilities, and fearful of getting involved with another man. I wanted to know, so I could help myself and others.

One of the most important things I learned is that there is a way out of the darkness. The trauma you have suffered is real, and you must work to heal yourself, but it is worth the effort. You can do this— you can get your confidence back, will smile again, and will even get to a point where you will want to meet someone new and start over. This book will take you through ten steps that will help you do just that. You'll learn about the reasons behind why your former partner treated you the way he did, if it's even possible to remain in a relationship with a narcissistic man, why he chose you, why it seems to hurt so bad, how to break it off, and steps to take to start healing yourself and creating the life that's right for you.

I understand how difficult that all might seem right now, but there is light at the end of this tunnel. You can emerge from the ashes of your toxic relationship, and make the choices that will cause your life to blossom into the beautiful flower it was always meant to be. I'll show you how to reimagine your life and become the best version of yourself. You can do it, and what's more, you deserve to have everything you've always dreamed of for your life. You don't have to stay trapped in a relationship with a psychopath, and you don't have to live the rest of your life as a celibate hermit either. I know it can seem like there's no way out or that you'll never want another relationship, but let me show you the way.

If you're reading this book, you're already looking for a better way. I know I was desperate to find that better path for myself. It's not always an easy road, but when you free yourself from the abuse you're suffering and begin to heal those wounds, you'll wonder why you ever doubted your own strength and determination. You'll discover just how strong you are, and you'll never fear striking out on your own again. You'll cultivate a deep understanding of your own self-worth as you realize you have the power to heal even the deepest of wounds. From there, you'll make the dreams you have for your life a lived reality, and yes, you'll find love again, and it will be sweeter still because you will know the value of self-love.

This is your time, the moment for you to reach for your star, your brass ring. To do that, you have to make the decisions that are best for you. You have to choose to become the best version of yourself, and to do that, you have to free yourself from the prison that narcissism built. My goal with this book is to help you start that journey by healing the wounds left behind by your toxic relationship. Come with me as we journey toward a better way. As Lao Tzu wrote, "A journey of a thousand miles begins with a single step." Take that step with me as we first seek to understand what creates a narcissist.

Chapter One: Toxic Relationships and Signs of Mental Abuse

Step 1: Understanding the psychological signs of abuse and how they can affect you

I don't want to get out of bed…

I remember that morning after coming back from Paris well. It was a grey and cold November morning. I didn't even want to open my eyes let alone start a new day. Truth be told, I didn't even know how to start that day, and I certainly didn't know to start my life over. My life was full of broken dreams and unfulfilled expectations. My family and business were destroyed, and the anxiety I was left with was destroying me from the inside, like a virus that was spreading. I just kept thinking, "I don't know how to live. I don't want to wake up. I don't want to get out of bed." It was all too much, so I slept until midday when I just couldn't sleep anymore.

I had to wake up and face the reality of being alone. For the next few days, I just existed. I had no desire to do anything other than sleep. I would wake up and wait for the night to arrive so I could go to sleep to avoid the terrible reality that was my life. There were many days like that, and even the pills I was taking for anxiety weren't working to help me calm down. I couldn't escape the fear I had inside. I couldn't hide from it, I couldn't get rid of it, and I was certain everyone could smell it on me. What should I do with my life? The only way I could respond was, "I will think about it tomorrow," just like Scarlett O'Hara in the famous movie, *Gone with the Wind*.

My sadness was profound, and I couldn't imagine I would ever feel better. I had already forgotten the last time I had smiled. I now lived with a new roommate named depression. I remember thinking, "Hello depression. We haven't met before, and I didn't invite you into my life, but now you are living with me." All I could do was accept the situation and sit with the feelings I was having. I needed time alone to recover, time for myself so I could heal from this wound. Would I someday think of this as a great life lesson? I chose to believe I would, but until then, I had to survive, and that meant I had to reinvent myself. How could I do that?

I decided to pamper the little girl—little Elena—who lived inside me. I would let her do whatever she felt like doing. For the first time in her life, she would be free to express her emotions and play. I would take care of her, and we would live in the present moment. The past was gone, and the future is a question mark. All I had was the present, and that's where I lived with my life on pause. But with time, and the techniques I will describe in this workbook, I began to dream again. My wounds began to heal, and I started to think about what I really wanted to do and how I wanted to move forward. This can happen for you too, and the first step is understanding when you're in a toxic relationship because when you name what you fear, you begin the process of conquering it.

Name the Beast to Tame the Beast: Signs of a Toxic Relationship

It's often very difficult to see the signs of a toxic relationship when you're still in one. Of course, you don't want to believe that the person you love would ever want to hurt you intentionally, but it's also true that when you're in love, you may look at everything through rose-colored glasses. You don't want to believe it's true, so you make up excuses for your partner, believe he will get better, or, in the worst-case scenario, you buy into the idea that you somehow deserved such bad treatment. It also isn't always so obvious when the relationship turns toxic. This is particularly true if you're not very experienced at being in a relationship.

Hollywood and other popular culture venues often portray abusive relationships differently than how they actually are reality. They may make them seem simply passionate or even extremely romantic. By showing them in this way, it becomes easy for people to normalize what is really unacceptable behavior. For example, if your partner says he can't live without you, that might seem romantic in a certain light, but it's really manipulative and often accompanied by very controlling behavior. It's a big red flag rather than an expression of love.

What is a Toxic Relationship?

Although you often hear this phrase used nowadays, the reality is that defining "toxic" can be tricky. It's a subjective term rather than a clinical one, and it can encompass a wide range of unhealthy behaviors. On one end of the spectrum, you might be two people who genuinely love one another, but who also argue a lot. On the other end of the spectrum, the situation could involve physical domestic abuse. The extremes are easy to understand, but the middle includes a lot of behaviors that aren't as clearly defined.

Of course, every relationship has problems, and after the rose is off the bloom, the behaviors of each partner can change somewhat. It's also true that every couple fights, and that's not really the issue with regard to a toxic relationship. It's not a situation of if you fight, but how. In general, in a healthy relationship, the good will outweigh the bad, but in a toxic relationship, the reverse is true; the bad far outweighs the good.

Additionally, if the relationship you're in is causing you to suffer from depression, hopelessness, or even occasionally suicidal thoughts, you are viewing signs of being in a toxic relationship. Your partner should be someone who makes you feel good about yourself. They should be your cheerleader and help you achieve your goals in life. They should care about how you feel and want you to be happy. That seems intuitive, but it can be hard to discern, so here are some concrete signs you're in a toxic relationship:

- **Your partner has no friends and doesn't want you to have any either**: Your relationship will be stronger if both of you have friends and other interests outside your relationship. However, a toxic partner is not only just toxic around you; they're also frequently toxic around other people. The difference is that his other friends won't stick around for long if they're treated like that. He also won't want you to have male friends or even go out with female ones. In fact, he might even demand that you should only engage in activities together. It's part of an isolation tactic; once you're isolated from other people, it can become more difficult to see that his behaviors are toxic.

- **Your partner leaves you feeling sick and tired**: If you're truly in love with someone, it will feel like you're walking on air, right? Unfortunately, with a toxic partner, it can feel like the weight of the world is on your shoulders. Every interaction leaves you feeling drained and anxious. This can even manifest into physical symptoms like a stomach ache, headache, or just feeling generally unwell. If this is something you're experiencing regularly, then it's a sign you're in a toxic relationship.

- **Your partner gets personal**: Everyone argues, but in a relationship, the key is in *how* you argue. If your partner respects you and your opinion, he will disagree respectfully and address the differences of opinion without resorting to personal attacks. If, on the other hand, he attacks you personally or calls you names, that's not a healthy way to argue. He might resort to name-calling, attacking your values, or even going after your physical appearance. These are toxic behaviors that can damage your relationship each and every time it happens.

- **Your partner constantly checks in with you**: Although you might send your partner a text once in a while throughout the day because you genuinely want to have him in your life as much as possible, a toxic husband or partner will use this tactic to try to control you. They might insist on tracking your location or demand that you text them at certain intervals. They might even demand that you send them pictures to prove where you are. They also might simply require you to reassure them of your devotion to them by constantly sending them messages when you're apart. These behaviors are both manipulative, controlling, and huge red flags for a toxic relationship.

- **Your partner talks too much or not enough**: A favorite trick of a toxic person is the silent treatment. The silent treatment is a passive-aggressive and disrespectful action in any relationship. It's never helpful to cut off lines of communication, and it's not healthy. How can you solve your problem if you don't talk about it? On the other end of the spectrum, the toxic partner will interrupt you constantly. That indicates they're not listening to you and don't really respect your thoughts or opinions.

In a healthy relationship, you would practice active listening with your partner. You would listen, accept that they believe what they're saying, repeat what you heard to confirm you understood correctly, and then respectfully state your opinion and reasons behind it. You might not arrive at a consensus in every situation either. You might have to agree to disagree, but you will understand one another on a deeper level as a result of respectful discussion.

- **You always apologize and aren't sure why**: Another favorite tactic of toxic partners is making you feel guilty. They will imply that you're responsible for their feelings with statements like, "You make me so angry!" Or, they'll make you feel guilty for your feelings or needs with statements like, "You're always so needy!" The truth is that you get to have your own feelings, needs, and desires. No one should make you feel guilty about them. In fact, a healthy partner will want to be sure your feelings are validated, your needs are met, and your desires are achieved. So, if you find that you're always apologizing for how your partner feels, your feelings, or for having desires or needs, that's another red flag that can indicate that the relationship is toxic.

- **Your partner wants you to change**: Your partner should love you exactly as you are, but a toxic man will want to fix you. They might want you to change your hair color, go on a diet, or even change your job. This is a sign they're trying to make you into what they want you to be instead of what you want to be. A healthy partner listens to what you want for yourself and helps you achieve your goals, and although each of you would have your flaws, you should work together to improve and inspire one another.

- **All of his exes are "crazy"**: Having one "crazy" ex isn't that unusual, but if *all* of his exes are crazy, then it's likely that the problem wasn't with them. Toxic people refuse to take responsibility for their actions and frequently will attack or blame anyone else but themselves. So, if they're trying to make it seem like they've always been the unfortunate one, that's a clue you might be in a toxic relationship.

- **He's obsessed with you**: It's easy to confuse obsession with love because it can feel so passionate. Of course, you want to be adored and even showered with gifts and attention. However, when love turns obsessive, it can lead to toxic behaviors like stalking, abuse, or jealousy, along with potentially other manipulative and controlling behaviors as well.

- **One or both of you has a substance abuse problem**: The abuse of alcohol or drugs goes hand-in-hand with toxic and abusive behavior. What's more, it can cause you to feel like you have to fix the problem, and you simply can't. The only person whose behavior you can change is yours, and if you've got a problem, you'll want to seek help for that too. You have to heal yourself before you can ever hope to heal your relationships. If you're in a toxic relationship, that likely means leaving it to get clarity on your problems and what it will take to heal them.

- **He lies even about the little things**: Another important sign of a toxic relationship is lying. In most toxic relationships, toxic partners don't just lie about the big things; they lie about little things too. Lying is a sign of disrespect, and it's a way of gaslighting you so you'll doubt your own feelings and experiences. It's also likely you'll soon find yourself hiding aspects of your relationships from loved ones or believing you need to lie to protect yourself or others. If that's happening, you're likely in a toxic relationship.

- **All of your friends hate him**: Sometimes your friends can see things you can't or don't want to see. It's one thing if your partner has problems with one of your friends, but if all of them are telling you the same thing, that could indicate that there's something you're not seeing. The behaviors associated with a toxic relationship can often be subtle when you're in the relationship. It might also be easy for you to explain away your partner's behavior, but your family and friends will have a more objective perspective. Furthermore, they have your best interests at heart, so it's worthwhile to listen to them. At least consider what they're saying and try to take an objective look at your relationship.

Personality Disorders and Toxic People

Aside from signs indicating that you're in a toxic relationship, it's also important to understand the kinds of problems that can cause your partner to engage in toxic behavior. One of the more common problems is narcissism. That's what my former husband had, but it's not the only cause of toxic behavior. It's part of a group of disorders known as personality disorders and specifically found in Cluster B. A personality disorder is characterized as a rigid, unhealthy pattern of thinking, behaving, and functioning. People with these disorders have trouble perceiving and relating to other people and situations, causing them to have significant problems forming healthy relationships, engaging in social activities, and performing well at work or school. Although no one is born with a personality disorder, once diagnosed, it cannot be completely cured.

On the other hand, a person might not even realize or acknowledge that they have a personality disorder, since they would only know their way of thinking, which would seem natural to them. As a result, they frequently blame other people for any challenges they face. They don't understand that the problem lies in their way of thinking and perceiving what's happening around them. For this reason, they can often have difficulty accepting responsibility for their role in causing problems. Personality disorders typically manifest in teenage or young adult years, and there are several types of these disorders. Some can become less obvious with age, though others persist at the same intensity for an individual's entire life.

Personality disorders are grouped into three clusters, and the disorders in each cluster share similar characteristics and symptoms. In fact, people who suffer from one personality disorder also tend to have another disorder from the same cluster. Let's begin by discussing the one I'm most familiar with, having lived through a relationship with someone who had this problem. It's important to remember that an individual doesn't have to display all of the symptoms to be diagnosed with one of these disorders.

Narcissistic Personality Disorder

Narcissism is normal to some extent in everyone and is necessary for a healthy self-esteem, but when they become extreme, they manifest as arrogance, condescension, and a superior attitude. If these behaviors are numerous and persistent, it's considered a personality disorder. Narcissism is categorized within Cluster B. Cluster B is composed of dramatism, unpredictability, and overly emotional thinking and behaviors. In our discussion of narcissism, it will be helpful to understand what causes this kind of disorder and its expression.

The kind of narcissism that most people think about when someone is identified as a narcissist is the unhealthy kind that has likely developed into a personality disorder. These individuals typically demonstrate at least five of the following traits:

- **A grandiose sense of self-importance**: They tend to exaggerate their achievements or talents and expect they will be recognized as superior, even without commensurate achievements.

- **Preoccupation with fantasies of power, success, brilliance, beauty, or ideal love**: They are obsessed with these concepts, and their behavior reflects that obsession.

- **Believe they are special or unique**: They feel they can only be understood by people they would consider a peer or higher status person, and they also believe they should only associate with unique people like themselves.

- **Require excessive admiration**: They expect and even need to be recognized for their achievements and admired for them.

- **Strong sense of entitlement**: They believe the world owes them and their expectations are that they will be treated favorably and people will automatically comply with their desires.

- **Exploit others**: They will take advantage of anyone to achieve their goals.

- **Lack empathy**: They simply cannot recognize or identify with other people's feelings or needs.

- **Envious of others**: They either envy those they think are superior to them, or they believe that everyone is envious of them. It is that envy that explains the criticism they receive.

- **Arrogant, haughty behaviors and attitudes**: They believe themselves to be superior and act accordingly.

Narcissism is defined as the tendency to consider oneself as superior, deserving, entitled, and unique or special, as well as having a propensity to demean, marginalize, and invalidate other people, so one can feel better about themselves. Narcissists come across as false and superficial; they judge others, are dismissive of their feelings and needs, and are completely self-absorbed. But what causes them to become that way?

Causes of Narcissism

There is no one cause for narcissism, and in fact, the reasons behind how this disorder forms are complicated and multi-faceted. Two common factors that psychologists often point to are what are known as the narcissistic wound and narcissistic indulgence. Most chronic narcissists have one or both of these factors even if they don't realize it. Let's look at each one.

Narcissistic Wound

The narcissistic wound develops as a result of at least one difficult life experience where the individual felt rejected, not accepted, or not good enough. Most of the time, this happens in their childhood and is combined with familial or social pressures that demand they be a certain way. In response to this pressure, the person develops a superficial, false persona that is contrary to their genuine self, and they do this so that they will be accepted and respected within their circumstances. This superficial persona is a way for them to avoid pain, hurt, and humiliation, and it helps them suppress feelings of shame or self-loathing.

Individuals with a healthy sense of self tend to respond to similar difficulties by harnessing their resiliency skills such as inner strength, a desire to grow and become a better person, or wanting to learn from their mistakes. Narcissists, on the other hand, employ these false schemes to compensate for their feelings. These schemes include their superficial persona, a desire for superiority, and a resistance to admitting their flaws and mistakes. When they use this mask—this false persona—they hope to get more attention, approval, and admiration while avoiding what they consider as a humiliation of being seen as a victim, which is what they perceive their real selves as.

Narcissists often speak about not wanting to be "looked down on," never feeling as though they are good enough, equating their worth as a person with their accomplishments, and being ashamed of their background. Their actions are a direct result of these feelings. They strive to have the material things they identify with success, marry people not because of love, but because they want to feel better about themselves, and make life choices based on the image those choices will project to others around them.

Although they believe the superficial mask will make them more acceptable, the opposite frequently happens instead, since they are still reacting out of a sense of inadequacy. The behaviors that result from that profound sense of self-loathing can create toxic and damaging relationships with others.

Narcissistic Indulgence

This refers to specific circumstances in the narcissist's family, social, educational, or professional lives that cause them to think they are, in fact, superior, special, better than others, or one of a kind. This leads them to believe they can do whatever they want and get away with it. They have likely never faced real criticism, breeding a sense of entitlement whereby the narcissist believes they deserve special treatment or more privilege. Moreover, they believe this should be granted without exception.

This type of narcissist often instigates misconduct and frequently treats others badly and with impunity. They abuse the positive circumstances they were given in life by presuming they have a natural right to be treated better than other people. They believe others should cater to their needs while they would have no responsibility to care for anyone else in their life. The world, they believe, revolves around them and their desires.

Although these indulgent narcissists project arrogance on the outside, the reality is that their self-esteem is precariously dependent on external circumstances and possessions. They have created a shell that portrays confidence while there is a hollow person who lacks any sense of meaningful purpose on the inside. They serve only their self-interest. They are plagued by insecurity and self-doubt as a result of basing their self-worth on superficial comparisons with others.

These narcissists are quick to anger if people don't respond promptly to their needs, a phenomenon known as narcissistic rage. They can't accept themselves simply as humans. If something happens to threaten their concept of superiority, their fragile self-esteem becomes threatened. Without the external trappings that they believe prove their inherent superiority, they crumble into a sense of unworthiness; they feel like a nobody.

Both causes of narcissism result in a lack of the capacity and/or willingness to even attempt to engage in healthy, loving, and truly equitable relationships. The people in their lives are there to be manipulated and exploited for their own selfish needs. They have little to no regard for the thoughts, feelings, or needs of others. They don't relate because they *can't* relate; instead, they use other people to further their own image.

Both wounded and indulgent narcissists often speak of being disappointed in the people around them—thinking of people as nothing more than numbers—and displeased if their needs are not met immediately. Can they change for the better? It's difficult and only possible if the narcissist is highly self-aware (a state that is almost impossible to reach for most narcissists) and courageous enough to engage in a journey of self-discovery. If they genuinely are no longer willing to roleplay at the cost of their integrity and authenticity in their relationships, then there are ways they can liberate themselves from their mask and begin the process of healing their wounds.

Other Cluster B Disorders

My experience was with a narcissist, but there are other disorders that result in toxic behaviors. Narcissism is but one Cluster B disorder. Others include antisocial personality disorder, borderline personality disorder, and histrionic personality disorder. They all have common symptoms and behaviors. The following sections will detail typical characteristics of each one.

Antisocial Personality Disorder

- Disregard for the feelings or needs of other people.
- Persistent lying, stealing, and conning of other people.
- Recurring problems with the law.
- Repetitive violation of other people's rights.
- Aggressive behavior, often to the point of violence.
- Disregard for their own safety and the safety of others.
- Impulsive behavior.
- Consistently irresponsible behavior.
- A lack of remorse for their behavior.

Borderline Personality Disorder

- Impulsive and often risky behaviors like unsafe sex, binge eating, or gambling.
- Fragile or unstable self-image.
- Intense, unstable relationships.
- Dramatic mood swings, particularly when subjected to interpersonal stress.
- Suicidal behavior or threatening to act on the ideation.
- Intense fear of abandonment.
- Persistent feelings of emptiness.
- Frequent, intense displays of anger.
- Intermittent stress-related paranoia.

Histrionic Personality Disorder

- Constant attention seeking behaviors.
- Excessive emotional, dramatic, or sexually provocative behaviors designed to gain attention.
- Expresses strong opinions in a dramatic fashion, but has few facts or details to help back them up.
- Easily influenced by other people.
- Rapidly changing and shallow emotions.
- Excessively concerned with their physical appearance.
- Believes their relationships with other people to be closer than they probably actually are.

One last definition to put in here—I have used the term *psychopath* in my books. I want to make clear that I am using this term colloquially rather than scientifically. There is, however, a correlation between narcissism and psychopathy. In fact, research has found that the two problems are both characterized by superficial charm, extreme arrogance, impulsivity, irresponsibility, and interpersonal duplicity.

As you can see, these behaviors are similar between the various disorders and can cause people to act out in toxic ways, particularly toward people with whom they are engaged in an intimate relationship. But, let's not kid ourselves; your behavior can contribute to the development of toxicity as well. It's a situation called codependency, and like personality disorders, many people don't recognize their own codependent behaviors.

Understanding Codependency

To understand the nature of a toxic relationship fully, you must also understand your role in perpetuating it. Codependency is also known as relationship addiction, and it is something you would learn from your family experiences as a child. From this perspective, it is a generational problem. Codependency was first used to describe partners in a relationship with someone addicted to drugs or alcohol, but the term has been broadened to include people in any dysfunctional family relationship. It describes an emotional and behavioral condition that affects your ability to have a healthy, mutually satisfying relationship.

A dysfunctional family is one where its members feel pain, anger, fear, or shame that they constantly ignore or deny. The underlying problems that might be causing these types of emotions include a family member struggling with addiction, the existence of physical, sexual, or emotional abuse in the family, and/or a family member who suffers from a mental or physical illness. The hallmark of a dysfunctional family is that they don't acknowledge the existence of such problems; instead, family members repress their emotions and come to disregard their needs. They survive the situation rather than confront and attempt to resolve it. This tends to cause detachment from the intrafamilial relationships wherein members don't talk, touch, confront, feel, or trust each other. Moreover, the attention and energy within the family is focused on the individual who is ill, and the other members sacrifice their own needs to care for that person.

Codependent people frequently have low self-esteem and often turn to external sources for validation and to feel better. That then often results in addiction to substances or compulsive behaviors. Although they have good intentions, they are simply unable to care for the person experiencing difficulties effectively. They might attempt to rescue the addict, for example, by paying to bail them out of jail, but their efforts simply result in enabling the destructive behavior. The codependent individual believes the person with problems needs them, and they then become compulsive in their efforts to care for them, resulting in them feeling as though they are helpless and have no choice in the relationship. Still, they also feel unable to break away from the cycle of behavior they have instigated. Ultimately, the codependent person views themselves as the victim.

Characteristics of a codependent person include:

- An exaggerated sense of responsibility.
- A tendency to confuse love and pity—they love the people they pity.
- A tendency to do more than their fair share every time.
- A tendency to feel hurt when the people they care for don't recognize their efforts and sacrifices.
- An unhealthy dependence on relationships, and they will do whatever is necessary to hold on to them so they don't feel abandoned.
- An extreme need for recognition and approval from other people.

- Feeling guilty when they assert themselves.
- A compulsive need to control other people.
- A lack of trust in themselves and others.
- Fear of abandonment.
- Difficulty identifying their own feelings.
- Difficulty adjusting to change.
- Difficulty setting boundaries and with intimacy.
- Chronic anger.
- Frequent lying and dishonesty.
- Poor ability to communicate.
- Problems making decisions.

Consequences of Toxic Relationships and Codependency

There are serious emotional and physical consequences of being involved in a toxic relationship. First, it's typical for toxic relationships to result in a psychological process called idealization. This is where your idea of the ideal partner—something rooted in your unconscious desires—has been influenced by either cultural or biological forces. These forces can keep you from seeing the red flags that are so obvious to the people around you. It's part of what can keep you in a relationship after it has turned toxic, but it also has real implications for your health.

For your mental health, a toxic relationship can cause you to feel insecure about yourself and develop low self-esteem. It can leave you feeling unhappy and drained from feeling pressured to change to meet the desires of your partner. There are also implications for your physical health. Studies have found that negative relationships can put you at a higher risk for developing heart problems, including a fatal heart attack. For women specifically, toxic relationships can result in high blood sugar levels, blood pressure, and rates of obesity. A toxic relationship can even slow down the healing of wounds.

Additionally, stress responses from your body— i.e., the constant stimulation of your fight or flight response—result in the overproduction of adrenaline, whereby the excess is then discarded. This can result in the fatigue of the system, possibly leading to a weakened immune system and organ damage. These are serious side effects that can ultimately shorten your life. That's part of why it's so critical that you work to free yourself from a toxic relationship. If the other person is not willing to work on the problem, then you have to take action to get out. The first step is understanding the nature of the problem.

An Exercise in Understanding

Now that you have a better idea of what constitutes a toxic relationship and how unhealthy narcissism can lead to toxic behavior, it's time to look at your own situation. Wherever you are in your relationship—whether you're still in one or you've left him—it's helpful to understand the nature of your experience. One of the best ways to gain valuable insight is to create a journal where you can safely reflect on what happened and the emotions that generated in you. Consider your journal as a trusted friend with whom you can share everything. Toward that end, buy a beautiful one for yourself that is inviting to write in, and that perhaps also has inspirational quotes to help motivate you to write often about your feelings. Specially for my readers I offer a special journal to this book, with all the exercises in it. You can get a printed version of this guided journal on Amazon that includes only exercises from this book and space for your notes.

This book will be your companion as you go through the healing process, so make it one that you will feel comfortable doing all of the exercises in this workbook in. As you write, allow yourself to write freely about what has happened to you. It can be helpful to structure your writing around answering certain questions. These are offered to get you started, but feel free to expand on any area or emotions that come up as you begin this process.

1. How did you meet your partner?

2. What was he like at first?

3. When did you first begin to believe there was a problem in your relationship?

4. What kinds of behaviors did you find hurtful or inappropriate?

5. How did those behaviors make you feel about yourself and your relationship?

6. Do you think your partner has a narcissistic personality disorder?

7. What kind of narcissistic behaviors does he display?

8. When did you start thinking about leaving your partner?

9. How does thinking about that make you feel?

10. What are your fears about leaving him?

As you write, allow yourself to just go with the flow of your thoughts. If you feel like writing about something not on this list, or if you go off in another direction, just let yourself express whatever you're feeling. By allowing yourself this type of free-flowing writing, you will gain valuable insights into your relationship and yourself. This can be very helpful when going through the healing process.

The next step in understanding your relationship is to identify if you're codependent. Try answering the following questions to identify codependency, but remember that codependency occurs on a spectrum whereby the intensity of symptoms may vary. That means you may not suffer from all of these symptoms, but you likely suffer from several of the indicators implied by the following questions:

1. Do you just not say anything about a problem because you don't want to get into an argument?

2. Do you worry about what other people will think about you?

3. Do you or have you ever lived with someone suffering from addiction?

4. Do you or have you ever lived with someone who either physically hit or emotionally belittled you?

5. Do you believe other people's opinions are more important than yours?

6. Do you find it difficult to adjust to changes occurring at work or in your home?

7. Do you think your partner is rejecting you if he spends time with his friends?

8. Do you doubt you can be the person you want to be?

9. Do you find it difficult to express your true feelings?

10. Do you or have you ever felt inadequate?

11. If you make a mistake, do you believe you're a bad person?

12. Do you find it's difficult to accept a compliment or gift?

13. If your child or spouse makes a mistake, do you feel humiliated?

14. Do you believe the other people in your life would go downhill if it weren't for your constant efforts?

15. Do you often wish that someone could help you get things done?

16. Do you find it difficult to talk to people in a position of authority, like your boss or the police?

17. Do you feel confused about who you are or where you are going with your life?

18. Do you find it difficult to say no when someone asks for help?

19. Do you find it difficult to ask for help?

20. Do you have so many different things going on at once, making it hard to give quality attention to any of them?

If you identify with several of these questions, that's a strong indicator that you're codependent. To find out for sure, you should seek professional help by arranging for a diagnostic evaluation with a licensed psychologist or physician who has experience in treating codependency. For our purposes here, however, if you have defined yourself as potentially codependent, write about your feelings around this insight. Was there someone in your childhood who modeled this for you? Do you think you came from a dysfunctional family? Let yourself express the feelings that come up freely as you answer these questions. Remember that your journal is your trusted friend, so tell it everything.

Once you have a full understanding of the behaviors that led to your toxic relationship, you can start healing and learning about developing healthy relationships. However, before moving on to that stage, it can help to discover why your toxic partner might have chosen you. We'll examine that next.

Chapter Two: Why Me? Who Psychopaths and Narcissists Choose to Target

Step 2: Introspection—what makes you a target for a narcissistic man

If you're in a relationship with a toxic man, or if you've just left such a relationship, it's not uncommon to wonder—why did he choose you? You might wonder if you've just got sucker written across your forehead or seem weak. The truth is that these toxic people often target partners for some of their *best* qualities, often because they want to destroy the very qualities they admire.

It's a common misconception that toxic people choose weak individuals to manipulate. In fact, they often prefer someone with a strong will rather than a weak one, since breaking and tearing them down will appear as a much bigger accomplishment in the end. Usually, whatever kind of strength a toxic man targets, they destroy, and it makes them feel better about themselves to have done so. The reasons behind this tactic involve the desire to feel good about themselves, and they can do that by being associated with someone who's successful and good or tearing someone down who seems to be mentally, physically, and emotionally strong. Along those lines, there are four general types of people that toxic individuals find to be attractive targets:

1. **Impressive people**: This might mean they are successful in their career, because of their talents and hobbies, or even because of their friends and family.

2. **People who make them feel good**: This might be because the person compliments the toxic person or gestures they make.

3. **Someone who makes the narcissist look good**: For a toxic person, it's all about the image they project, and if you can enhance their image, that would make you a target.

4. **Someone who validates their feelings**: Toxic people are highly attracted to those who can overlook the toxic person's flaws and validate

their feelings. This reassures them that their target won't leave them when they fly into a rage.

Most toxic men also have unrealistic expectations for their partner. What's more is that they have unstable object constancy, which basically means they have difficulty maintaining a positive emotional bond with someone when they also feel hurt, angry, or disappointed in them. If you're a healthy person, you can separate them from their behavior; you can love them despite the fact that they did something you don't like. However, for a toxic person, that is not something that comes easily. Additionally, object constancy pertains to staying emotionally connected to your partner, even when they're not around physically. This results in that narcissistic rage, for example, that you might experience in a toxic relationship.

It's also true that most toxic men are interested in controlling you. They want to have power over their partner, and one way they can gain that power is to destroy their healthy partner. So, what kind of traits exactly do toxic men look for in that partner? You might be surprised to see these positive traits, but remember that to the toxic man, they indicate someone over whom they can gain control.

- **Forgiving**: Someone who is forgiving is just the perfect victim for the toxic abuser who takes delight in hurting their partner. They need someone who doesn't hold a grudge and can forgive them when they fly into a rage.

- **Loyal**: This is another positive quality that the toxic man looks for in a target. They need someone who will feel like they need to stick it out. They also want someone who will be loyal to them, despite how they won't be loyal back. Toxic men will often betray the relationship with no remorse.

- **Overlooks bad qualities**: Toxic men want someone who will overlook their bad qualities and only see the good in other people. It's not uncommon for someone like this to focus on the positive traits of their partner while ignoring the bad things they do. The toxic man needs this because their behaviors will become increasingly bad.

- **Have an "external locus of control"**: This refers to people who are self-referencing versus other-referencing. Someone who is self-referencing considers how they feel internally about something before making a decision, whereas someone who is other-referencing is focused on how the decision they make will make other people feel. For that reason, someone who is other-referencing has their locus of control located externally, making them a perfect target for all types of emotional abusers.

- **Self-sacrificing**: Normally, you would consider this to be a noble characteristic, but for a toxic man, they need a partner who sacrifices their own needs for those of their partner. This will make the toxic partner believe they will always have someone to take care of them—someone who is willing to focus solely on the toxic man's needs.

- **Overly responsible**: Toxic men typically target people who take on the responsibilities of others without even realizing it. Most toxic men are irresponsible in their actions, so having someone who is willing to pick up the pieces is just perfect for them. They want someone to take care of the practical side of life, so they don't have to be concerned with it themselves.

- **Accommodating**: Narcissists and other toxic people are all about having their own way— they are inflexible, rule-oriented, and controlling. It's helpful to them to have someone who's willing to go with the flow and accommodate their rules. Toxic men look for those who are willing to compromise and accommodate the needs and desires of their narcissistic partner.

- **Unstable self-esteem:** Toxic men prey on people with unstable or low self-esteem because these are precisely the people over whom they can gain control. They are very manipulative, and if you have a low self-esteem, it makes you more vulnerable to the manipulative behavior that is so typical of toxic men.

When a narcissist finds someone with these characteristics, they will marshall all their charms to hook their victim. Narcissists often have considerable charms in the short term. They will frequently rush the progress of their relationship, however, so they can settle into the life they want to have and finally reveal their true self. The truth generally comes as a surprise to the narcissist's partner; they often can't believe the change that has occurred in how their partner is behaving, but when they see that the situation won't change, they often decide to break free.

If you've broken away from a toxic relationship, you might be kicking yourself while figuring out why you stuck around as long as you did or how you even allowed someone so toxic in your life in the first place. But the thing is that the whole reason the toxic man targeted you in the first place is because of your strengths, qualities of kindness and compassion, and desire to consider the needs of others. These psychological abusers are attracted to people who are successful, have good friends, or have lots of money, so they can either destroy those qualities or use them to boost their own self-esteems. These toxic men want to destroy you so they can feel better about themselves and often focus on finding certain traits. Understanding why can help you gain insight into your own situation.

- **Relationships with family and friends**— Narcissists and other psychological abusers want to isolate you from anyone who can restore your confidence or inspire you to be your best, which could eventually mean you can move on from your abuser. Do that, and they will often attempt to cause issues from within. They will begin by showing excitement and desire to be a part of those relationships, but then, as it happened in your relationship with them, they will become overly critical of your friends and family. This divide can cause your friends and family to pull away from you to stop the emotional abuse that they are also experiencing.

- **Your success**—Toxic men will target any area of your life where you have experienced success. That might mean your career, physical health, or financial stability. These are all things that can build your self-esteem, which are all dangerous to the narcissist. If you're confident in yourself and have a good sense of self-worth, you're not likely to put up with the mental abuse coming from your narcissistic partner. Such abusers don't want you to have success; they would prefer that you were dependent on them. Because you're probably someone who doesn't assume that others are out to hurt you, it can be easy to become a target of this kind of manipulation. When you find someone you're in love with, you will naturally want to share your success.

You might not be accustomed to thinking about how to protect the things you've worked hard to accomplish, but it's necessary no matter what your situation is, and it's particularly critical if you are in a toxic relationship. To protect yourself, you must set strong boundaries so you can resist the manipulative behavior of your partner. If they don't want you to go to the gym to stay physically fit, you have to resist the urge to listen and go anyway. You also need to realize that someone who isn't a controlling individual wouldn't be concerned with you staying fit, and in fact, they would *encourage* you to stay healthy. The fact that your partner is trying to keep you from your usual routine is a big red flag.

Why Are Empaths So Often Targeted by Toxic Men?

Empaths are a common target of those with Cluster B personality disorders. Perhaps it's because they are opposites in so many ways, and toxic people want to destroy that opposite. In the case of the toxic man, however, the attraction is for all the wrong reasons. Toxic abusers are looking to get the most out of their target—they are attracted to people who will validate their feelings and make them feel good. By that logic, empaths are *exactly* what they're looking for.

Toxic men thrive on their need for admiration, but they have no empathy for other people. Empaths are highly sensitive to the emotions of other people. In fact, they're emotional sponges, meaning they absorb the feelings of other people. To a toxic man, this kind of person can fulfill their every need and will do so selflessly. However, this kind of attraction is also destined for disaster.

In the empath, the toxic man sees someone who is giving and loving, and someone who will be devoted and willing to listen to their problems, needs, and goals in life. The problem is that those qualities aren't returned. Toxic men are presenting nothing more than a facade—a false self—to the empath. They are capable of seeming charming and compassionate at first, but that won't last long. Before long, they'll show their true face, including their cold, withholding, and punishing side. This is something that is very damaging to the empath.

Narcissists and other toxic men often begin to show their true faces when they notice their partner's flaws. Because these toxic men are full of contempt and self-loathing while projecting a facade of perfection, when they realize their partner is not perfect, they will stop idealizing them and start blaming them. They wanted the perfect partner to make them look good, and a flawed partner can't do that for them. Although it takes a while to show their true colors, when they do, it can be devastating for the empath.

The empath desires to help and heal people with compassion. They have a tendency to think that if they just listened or gave more to the relationship, their partner would change. They would feel more secure and loved, and that would make all the difference. However, that just isn't true with a narcissist. Even so, the empath can't bring themselves to believe that it's possible for a person to be lacking in empathy, and they can't believe their love won't heal them.

For their part, the toxic man *thrives* on drama and chaos, which is the opposite of what the empath works to achieve. They want harmony and peaceful coexistence. The toxic man desires exactly the opposite of that, making them the perfect target. Narcissists and other toxic men are easily able to manipulate empaths. They string them along with hope by integrating compliments and kindness in their behavior. That makes the empath believe that they can get that loving person they first fell in love with back with good behavior. They patiently try to do just that.

Empaths tend to believe that everyone is human and has flaws, and that belief fuels their patience. Toxic men can see that hope and will often tell them that they really do want to change. This statement encourages the empath to believe that change is possible. The narcissist may even agree to work on their flaws, but they never really follow through on those promises. It's nothing more than a tactic they use to keep the empathic partner hooked. They know that the empath wants to support and help them grow, but the toxic man is just looking to exploit the situation further.

Trauma Bond

A relationship with a toxic man can generate what is called a trauma bond, which can make it feel impossible to leave. A trauma bond forms when you're involved in a rollercoaster relationship like that which is typical of one with a toxic man. In such a tumultuous relationship, the target is barraged with a mix of insults and love bombs. Your body responds by producing high levels of cortisol when you're being insulted, and when the love bomb hits, your body produces a shot of dopamine as a kind of reward for your accommodating behavior. When this happens repetitively, it's like forming a bad habit. It's the same kind of thing your body goes through when you're addicted to a drug, and, just like an addiction, it can be difficult to quit the habit.

Added to the mix when the relationship involves an empath is how empaths are willing to look at themselves and their own faults. That fact plays into the formation of the trauma bond. When an empath is trauma-bonded, they examine their own behavior to see what they can do to change themselves so their partner will change. They look at their own flaws, but they're not as quick to look at the flaws of their partner. It can be difficult for the empath to understand that they are only responsible for their own growth; they have to let other people be responsible for theirs too.

The empath, no matter how loving and empathic they are, cannot do the work that others have to do to heal themselves. It's difficult for them to let other people go through suffering, causing significant change to begin. They literally feel the suffering of their partner and want to do what they can to help them heal. This makes it imperative that empaths make themselves adept at setting and maintaining strong boundaries. That can be hard for them to do because they often interpret it as being hard-hearted. They need to become more adept at it, however, since not everyone is healthy for them, and they have to learn to let those kinds of people go. Everyone has their own path in life, including the toxic man. Only they can heal themselves, and only they can make the choice to make real changes in their life. For the empath—or any other victim of the narcissist—they too will likely need to embark on a journey of self-healing.

Introspective Exercise

For this next exercise, look inward and honestly assess not only what it is about yourself that made you the target of the toxic man, but what it is that prevented you from stopping the abusive treatment. To begin, answer the following questions and write about any emotions they invoke in your journal:

1. Are you an empath?

2. Do you tend to put the needs of others ahead of your own?

3. Do you tend to consider how others might react as a result of your decisions?

4. If you answered yes, how does that affect the decisions you make?

5. Are you loyal to a fault?

6. Do you tend to take on the responsibilities of other people as though they were your own?

7. Are you someone who makes your narcissistic partner look good?

8. Does he use you to boost his own image?

9. Does he listen when you talk about your desires and needs?

10. How does it make you feel if he doesn't?

As with before, feel free to let your writing flow in any direction you feel compelled to write about. Take the time to really understand your feelings around these questions. What comes up for you as you write? Do you feel angry, ashamed, or like a fool? If you harbor such feelings about what happened, think about the kinds of boundaries you could have set that would have made a difference in how the situation played out. List at least five boundaries you could have set and how they would have changed things. Perhaps they would have allowed you to see what was happening sooner, or maybe they would have prevented you from getting in any deeper. Commit to establishing those boundaries in any future relationships by creating one positive affirmation for each boundary as well. Consider the following examples:

Boundary: I will pursue my interests, regardless of what else is going on in my life.
Affirmation: I am deserving of the success I achieve in every area of my life.

Boundary: I won't tolerate personal insults in an argument.
Affirmation: I am deserving of respectful treatment in all of my relationships.

Boundary: I will not give up my friendships and family relationships for anyone.
Affirmation: I am deserving of loving friends and strong, positive family ties.

Once you've developed your five boundaries and affirmations, commit to repeating those affirmations at least three times a day—three times for each affirmation. This will actually change the physical pathways in your brain, and positive thinking will become your habit.

Chapter Three: Complex Post-Trauma Stress Symptoms

Step 3: Diagnosing your trauma—C-PTSD symptoms in women

Post-traumatic stress disorder, or PTSD, is caused by some type of traumatic event. You've probably heard about it associated with war veterans, but it can also be caused by physical assaults, rape, car accidents, or emotional abuse. Really, any kind of disturbing or upsetting event that occurs can result in PTSD, particularly if it overwhelms your ability to cope with what happened. What's more, women are twice as likely to suffer from PTSD, and they also experience a longer duration of symptoms and more sensitivity to any triggers that remind them of the event. PTSD, as you've probably commonly heard of it, happens after a single traumatic incident, but there is another form, called Complex PTSD or C-PTSD, that results from repeated trauma over months or years. This is the type of PTSD we'll be talking about, though both types of PTSD share similar symptoms and treatments.

The effects of C-PTSD can be drastic if left untreated, and aside from the mental health implications of the condition, it can also lead to physical health problems too. You might suffer from headaches, stomach problems, and sexual dysfunction, among other things. What happens with C-PTSD is that you're not only remembering what happened; it's as if you're back in the incident you endured. It's like you went back in time and are living through that moment again. Your body responds as if you are too, and in response to it, the body produces the stress hormones that result in a whole range of physical, mental, and emotional symptoms.

C-PTSD in Women

Women who are suffering from the effects of C-PTSD often don't seek help, sometimes for years, and then, when they do, the condition is frequently misdiagnosed or missed altogether by the health professional. Many doctors don't have the proper training or experience to recognize and treat C-PTSD. It is also not uncommon that the woman herself may not be aware of the problem.

Women tend to internalize their problems, and rather than look outward to their situation, they might just decide that what they're suffering from is just a product of their own personality, thoughts, and emotions. They don't realize that there is a concrete problem from which they're suffering. For that reason, it's important to understand the causes, symptoms, and treatments for this condition. It's hard though because there is still a stigma against most mental health disorders, and that's particularly true for women who suffer from PTSD following an assault, or C-PTSD following years of emotional abuse. Moreover, women are frequently traumatized further by the professionals in whom they confide. They might be questioned about the veracity of what they're saying and their reaction to the situation.

Differences in PTSD and C-PTSD Between Men and Women

As with many diseases and conditions, there is a difference in how women experience C-PTSD compared to men. Women, for example, are more likely to experience depression and anxiety, while also having more difficulty feeling and dealing with their emotions. Additionally, they often avoid activities and things that remind them of what happened to them. On the other hand, men are more likely to turn to alcohol or drugs to mask their emotional response to trauma. Women are less likely to do that.

The key to treating C-PTSD is to be educated about how it can affect you. It is a treatable condition, but you first have to recognize that you have a problem. This can be difficult for women since they frequently feel a need to be perfect and are often reluctant to admit they have something that they perceive as a weakness. It's not just their perception either; women are constantly told they need to do it all and must do it well. That's an unrealistic expectation, and can create rather intense pressure. Before we talk about some of the treatment options for C-PTSD, let's look at some of the more common symptoms for both women and men.

C-PTSD Symptoms

For C-PTSD to be diagnosed, a patient must experience symptoms for at least a month, though they could be suffering for months or years before going for a diagnosis. Symptoms might not appear immediately, either. When they do, they can typically be categorized into three types:

1. Re-experiencing the trauma, which typically occurs in the form of intrusive and distressing recollections of a single event or multiple events. These recollections could come in nightmares or through flashbacks.

2. Emotional numbness and avoidance of places, people, or activities that remind the individual of what happened to them.

3. Increased arousal, which can result in difficulty concentrating or sleeping, as well as feeling jumpy and being easily irritated and angered.

Typically, the traumatic events that cause PTSD, in general, include exposure to actual or threatened death, serious injury, or sexual violation, but trauma also occurs with long-term emotional abuse, where the individual's fight or flight response was repeatedly stimulated, eventually resulting in complex-PTSD. In this situation, the brain doesn't distinguish between physical trauma and emotional trauma; it only reads your fear and responds accordingly. It also tends to read anxiety as fear and responds with a cascade of physiological responses, including the production of stress hormones. As we've already discussed, the chronic production of stress hormones has dramatic physical and emotional effects. It's also important to note that the threat or abuse doesn't have to be directed at the individual involved, and both kinds of PTSD can also result when someone witnesses a traumatic event or emotional abuse. The specific symptoms for a diagnosis in each of these general categories include the following:

Re-Experiencing the Trauma

Re-experiencing trauma can take the following forms:

- Spontaneous, recurrent, and involuntary memories of the traumatic event that intrude into an individual's consciousness. For example, experiencing a memory can happen when a trigger is perceived. In children, this might be seen in how they play. Their play may take the form of themes or aspects of the trauma they suffered.

- Recurrent and distressing dreams related to the traumatic event. This might mean dreaming specifically about the event, but it can also just be dreams that have a feeling similar to it. In children, this may take the form of dreams that don't have any recognizable content.

- Dissociative reactions—such as flashbacks—where the individual experiences the memory as if it were actually happening again. This typically causes the individual to become fully immersed in the flashback. In children, this might be seen as specific trauma reenactments during play.

- Intense, prolonged psychological distress from being exposed to either internal or external triggers that symbolize the traumatic events.

- Specific physiological reactions to reminders of the trauma they suffered. For example, some individuals might become nauseated when stimulated by a reminder of what they suffered.

Avoidance of Distressing Memories

This is a more typical response for women and can be diagnosed based on the presence of two or more of the following symptoms:

- An inability to remember certain important aspects of the traumatic event that cannot be accounted for by a head injury, alcohol, or drugs.

- Persistent and often exaggerated negative beliefs or expectations about oneself, other people, or the world in general. For example, the person might say, "I am bad," "No one can be trusted," or "The world is a dangerous place."

- Persistent feelings of self-blame or blaming others regarding what caused the consequences of the traumatic events.

- Persistent feelings of fear, horror, anger, shame, or guilt.

- Diminished interest in participating in significant activities.

- Feeling detached or estranged from other people.

- A persistent inability to experience positive emotions.

Changes in Arousal and Reactivity

This can occur in both men and women and can be diagnosed based on two or more of the following changes:

- Irritability and a marked increase in aggression.

- Reckless or self-destructive behavior.

- Hypervigilance.

- An exaggerated startle response.

- Problems concentrating.

- Difficulty falling or staying asleep, as well as restless sleep.

- Significant distress or impairment in social or occupational areas of functioning that cannot be attributed to the effects of medication, drugs, alcohol, or some kind of medical condition like a traumatic brain injury.

Treatment Options for PTSD and C-PTSD

There are several treatment options available for both kinds of PTSD that have been shown to be effective for helping women cope with their symptoms. These include both psychological and medication-based treatments. The first step in treating PTSD (either kind), however, is to diagnose the condition. To diagnose PTSD, your doctor will begin with a physical examination to check for any medical problems that might be related to your symptoms; this is to rule out the possibility that your symptoms are caused by other conditions and not PTSD. Once those physical ailments are ruled out, the doctor may refer you to a psychologist for an evaluation. That will involve discussing your symptoms and the events that likely produced them. Finally, the psychologist will make use of the diagnostic criteria listed in the Diagnostic and Statistical Manual of Mental Disorders (DSM-5).

A diagnosis requires that you were exposed to trauma either directly, as a witness, or through learning someone close to you was traumatized. Additionally, you might have been repeatedly exposed to graphic details of a traumatic event, as might be the case with first responders. Along with exposure to the trauma of some kind, your symptoms must have been persistent for more than one month, and they must create significant problems in your ability to function in the different areas of your life.

Once a diagnosis has been made, the treatment can begin with normalizing the symptoms and experiences of the individual struggling with the problem. Normalizing involves the following:

- Recognizing and accepting that physical pain may be a symptom. People with either kind of PTSD can struggle with migraines, back pain, or stomach and digestive issues.

- Recognizing and accepting that flashbacks or nightmares might occur and that they can be triggered by sounds, smells, or even a phrase that someone else says.

By normalizing the symptoms, it can help alleviate the patient's sense of guilt. The treatment is still a long process, but it begins with hope. The goals of the treatment program include helping you regain a sense of control over your life by utilizing the following strategies:

- Teaching skills to address the symptoms as they occur.
- Helping you think more positively about yourself, other people, and the world in general.
- Learning better coping strategies for symptoms.
- Treating other symptoms related to the traumatic experience, like depression, anxiety, or substance abuse.

Psychotherapy

There are several types of psychotherapies that can help treat children and adults with this condition. Some forms of psychotherapy include the following:

1. **Cognitive Therapy**: This form of therapy helps you identify your patterns of thinking—also known as cognitive patterns—that are keeping the trauma stuck in your body. You might have, for example, some negative core beliefs about yourself that the traumatic experience triggered in you. You could also be experiencing negative beliefs about your own self-worth and the possibility of traumatic events happening again in the future. You might believe, for example, that you deserved to have those bad things happen to you. This treatment strategy is often done in conjunction with exposure therapy.

2. **Exposure Therapy**: This style of therapy helps you face the memories and situations that you find frightening safely, so you can utilize new coping strategies to deal with them more effectively. This is a strategy that is particularly effective for flashbacks and nightmares. It often even uses innovative technology, such as virtual reality programs, to help you re-enter the setting in which you

had originally experienced the trauma. This form of therapy is most often used with veterans suffering from PTSD.

3. **Eye Movement Desensitization and Reprocessing (EMDR)**: This combines exposure therapy with a repetitive series of guided eye movements to help you process those traumatic memories, thus helping you change your reaction to them.

Through the use of these therapy styles, you can develop better stress management coping strategies that can help you handle stressful experiences. They can help you regain a sense of control over those lingering fears following traumatic experiences. The specific therapy or combination of therapies is something each individual must discuss with their mental health professional. In addition, you will often have the choice to engage in individual therapy, group therapy, or both, and there are benefits to each. In individual therapy sessions, you can get individualized attention and treatment, but in group therapy, you can meet other people who have been through similar trauma, which in itself will also be a valuable experience.

Medication

It could also be necessary to use medication to help with some of the symptoms of PTSD. The choice of medication includes the following:

- **Antidepressants**: Antidepressants are effective in treating both depression and anxiety, which can help improve both your sleeping and concentration. Common medications include selective serotonin reuptake inhibitors (SSRI) like Zoloft and Paxil. These have been approved by the Food and Drug Administration (FDA) for the treatment of PTSD.

- **Anti-anxiety medications**: These drugs can help relieve severe anxiety and any problems that result from that. These are generally only used in the short term; however, since several forms of anti-anxiety medication are addictive and easy to abuse.

- **Prazosin**: This drug, also known as Minipress, can help alleviate or suppress nightmares in certain people diagnosed with PTSD.

As with psychotherapy, if you and your doctor decide that you would benefit from medication, you'll have to work together to determine which medication will be best for your specific symptoms and situation. You will want to choose a drug that will have the fewest side effects, provide relief from your symptoms, and boost in your mood as soon as possible, hopefully within a few weeks. You should always be candid with your doctor about any other medications you currently take, if you are using drugs, or if you drink alcohol regularly. Some medications can interact with other substances. It's also a good idea to bear in mind that you may need a combination of medications, and it can take a while to determine the correct dosage for each that is right for you.

For my particular situation, I experienced C-PTSD as a result of a combination of traumatizing treatment and how the sudden change in my husband's personality and behavior left me doubting my ability to judge the character of another person. I thought the world was one way, and it turned out that it was something completely different. That distorted my reality and left me feeling doubtful that I could spot those kinds of situations going forward. It made me feel kind of paralyzed in my life—as though I was stuck in one place. I couldn't see how to move forward since my self-confidence had been shattered both by his emotionally abusive treatment of me and my perceived failure to see it.

It's strange how our culture often makes us feel as though if we get fooled by someone and that we are to blame. But why is that? Why am I to blame because someone else chooses to lie or hides their true character? Why am I expected to know? Prior to this experience, I had bought into the idea that I was adept enough at judging people's basic character. Of course, my toxic husband was also very adept at hiding his true self, and he pursued me relentlessly. He was utterly charming in the beginning, and there was no reason for me to think that he was anything other than what he seemed to be. Then, the rug was pulled out from under me. I felt responsible somehow, and it was only after intense treatment that I was able to regain my confidence and move forward with my life.

You are not to blame for what has happened to you. You might be codependent, but that doesn't make you responsible for the behaviors of someone who would take advantage of that fact. I learned this through regular therapy sessions, where I could explore my feelings and work through some of my personal core beliefs. You can do this too. But let's start with another exercise that can help you identify your PTSD symptoms.

Exploration Exercise

Let's begin by describing what you have experienced with your toxic partner. What were the kinds of things he said or did to you that made you realize you were in a toxic relationship? Before you begin writing about what you experienced, it's important to become aware of your body. Both kinds of PTSD often manifest with both physical and emotional symptoms. Begin by sitting in a relaxed position, but one in which you can write. Before you begin writing, close your eyes and take a series of deep breaths that expand your belly. Bring your attention to your body and notice how it feels. Are there any areas of aches or pains? If so, bring your focus to those areas and notice how the pain feels. Is it sharp or dull? Constant or intermittent? What is its intensity level? Breathe into those areas of pain and notice if it helps to ease it at all. Take a few more deep breaths and open your eyes, then begin writing.

1. Document your experiences. Be as detailed as possible, but while you are engaged in this process, notice any physical symptoms that arise and document them too. Do you feel a headache coming on? Does your stomach tighten as you recall the events to which you were exposed? Make notes of any symptoms you experience along with what you were documenting when they happened.

2. Next, answer the following questions regarding your symptoms:

    a. Do you have recurrent nightmares?

    b. Do you experience flashbacks where you feel as though you're in the situation again?

    c. Do you avoid places, activities, people, or anything else that might remind you of the situation you were in?

    d. Do you frequently feel anxious or nervous?

    e. Do you avoid going out in public?

    f. Do you find yourself feeling depressed and alone?

    g. Do you engage in risky behaviors like driving fast, gambling, substance abuse, or any other kind of self-destructive behavior?

As you answer these questions, try to be as detailed as possible. Additionally, notice any changes you feel in your body. Sometimes, your body may react in subtle ways; for example, you might find yourself getting tired suddenly. This might be your body trying to distract you from the thoughts and emotions you're provoking. You might suddenly become very uncomfortable and have the urge to get up and move around. That's another distraction technique to keep you from confronting some difficult emotions. When these distractions arise, try sitting with them for a few minutes without doing anything to alleviate them. You'll likely notice that the feelings change when you don't respond immediately. Document everything you experience, as these will help you understand your symptoms fully.

The truth is that you will have to sit with the difficult emotions before all of this is over, but as you do, you can notice how they shift. Believe it or not, by sitting with them, you'll help move them out of your body. When you do that, you'll be on your way to overcoming your PTSD.

Chapter Four: Why Does it Hurt So Much? Breaking Away from the Emotionally Abusive Relationship

Step 4: Understanding why breaking up with a toxic man can be so difficult

I couldn't believe how much I was hurting when I left my ex. The way I felt about what I had been through made me think I would be so happy to be out of the relationship, but that's not what I felt. I was incredibly sad, depressed, insecure, and I couldn't begin to picture myself in another relationship. I also couldn't see how I was going to get my life back together. It was so different from how I expected to feel. Prior to the experience, I would also wonder why women would stay in an abusive relationship. I'm sure many wonder the same thing about why I stayed as long as I did. You also might commonly hear people saying things like, "I would never put up with that." I also thought those things, and suddenly, there I was putting up with the very things I had told friends I would never stand for. Well, it's a whole different story when you're going through it yourself, but why is it hard for people to leave their partners, even if the relationship is abusive?

Why She Stayed—Personal Reasons

Let's take a closer look at why so many women stay in abusive relationships and may still even love their ex-partner after they've left. As the saying goes, it's complicated. However, there are reasons why you might still feel love for someone after leaving them. Here are a few:

- **Love doesn't disappear overnight**: You made a strong emotional connection with your partner, and when that connection was first formed, it's likely they weren't acting abusive. It's not easy to just let go of those feelings or that connection. You put a lot of time, energy, and trust into the life you built with him, and even though he is abusive, it's still hard to just give that all up.

- **You remember the good times**: Another factor in letting go is that you continue to remember the good times in your relationship. Abuse usually doesn't begin right away in a relationship; rather, it escalates slowly over time. In the beginning of your relationship, he was likely on his best behavior. He was probably charming, thoughtful, complimentary, and supportive. That's how my ex was. The emotional abuse began slowly, and it took some time before he became controlling. It can be difficult to believe that the abusive behavior you're seeing really represents how your partner is, and by the time you do believe, your lives have likely become so entangled that leaving is no longer a matter of merely walking out the door.

It's also true that no one is all good or all bad. It can be hard to leave even an abusive partner if you can see their good qualities as well. You might be so in love with them for the person they could be, and that can make it hard to see the person they *are*. It's easy to convince yourself that you can somehow reason with your partner and get them to act better; that if you just say the right words, they'll see the error of their ways and things will turn around. You might also experience long periods of calm in your relationship and might reason that you can put up with the occasional abuse, but that's an illusion. The reality is that your partner will likely become more controlling over time, and unless they seek help for their problems, the abuse is not only likely to continue, but it will probably escalate as well. Moreover, the abuse is not your fault, and thus, nothing you say or do can prevent it. It doesn't have anything to do with you; it's your partner who has a problem.

- **You see your partner's trauma**: It's true that many people who are abusive in relationships

224

are that way because they have also been traumatized at some point in time. You care about this person, and you might think that you can help them heal from their own trauma. You might think that putting up with the abuse is okay and you can try to help "fix" them. The problem with this kind of thinking is that you can't fix another person; you can only fix yourself, and your partner can only fix himself. That's a significant point to understand because no matter what caused the trauma your ex might be going through— whether it be mental illness, addiction, or their own abusive past—they must choose to seek help, and even if they do, there's never an excuse for them to abuse you or anyone else. They *choose* to keep doing so, and they *choose* not to seek help for their behavior. That is not your fault, and you have a right to not be abused.

- **Love as a survival technique**: Another factor that comes into play is that many victims of abusive partners use the love they have for their abuser to survive. It's difficult if you're not abusive to think that someone you love and who loves you would ever harm or mistreat you. In your mind, they would never want to see you hurt because you are not an abuser and would never want to see someone you love hurt. So, to cope with how they are

225

harming you, it often happens that you can detach from the pain of that fact by subconsciously seeing everything from your partner's perspective. In other words, you start to agree with their reasons for abusing you. They may tell you that they yelled at you because you were nagging them, and you may start to think, "Well, I was nagging, and I'm sure that's annoying, so I can see why they yelled at me and said those cruel things."

It's common for abusive people to blame the victim. They are often claiming that "She made me do it by arguing with or nagging me." If your abuser uses these techniques, he is manipulating you by distorting your reality, a technique also known as gaslighting. If you start to agree with him, his manipulation will only get worse because it's having the exact effect he wants it to have. You're simply learning how to appease him, and in the process, you're losing your personality and perspective. That's survival mode, and it can lead to you becoming even more dependent on your abuser. You might love this person, and if you do, you will most certainly want to believe they can change and will do so because they love you too. It's okay to want to believe them and for them to change, but it's not okay for them to continue abusing you.

- **The abuse destroys your self-esteem**: The longer you stay in an abusive relationship, the more your self-esteem will suffer. I wasn't in my relationship all that long, but as soon as the abuse ramped up, I started doubting myself and believing that maybe I had provoked him or I wasn't as capable as I had previously thought. It happens fast, and this kind of emotional abuse is every bit as destructive as physical abuse. When someone is constantly making you believe you're worthless or stupid, it's easy to start thinking that you'll never be able to find someone else if you leave. Take it from me—that's simply not true. There is a life free from abuse waiting for you, and you deserve to have it.

- **The cycle of abuse has a lovely make-up phase**: After every incident of abuse, it's common for abusers to tell you how much they love you, shower you with attention and compliments, and promise never to act that way again. The good times can be so good that you're willing to put up with the bad times. However, here's the thing—you should *never* have to put up with bad times. There's no trade-off worth the abuse.

- **It can be dangerous to leave, very dangerous**: It can literally be life-threatening to leave some abusive relationships, even if your partner has never physically abused you. In fact, women are as much as 70 times more likely to be killed in the first few weeks after leaving an abusive partner than at any other time in their relationship. So, the post-breakup period is a dangerous time when the relationship involves an abusive partner. Remember that it's all about power and control, and when you've finally broken free, your ex-partner might then go to extremes to exercise that control and power. That's why it's important to minimize contact after breaking up and be sure you can live in a safe place. Of course, if your partner was both physically and emotionally abusive, you'll want to take legal steps to prevent him from coming around you or any children the two of you may have. That means securing a restraining order, finding a safe house to stay where your partner can't find you, and securing sole custody of any children.

- **It's hard to escape the cycle of control**: It takes an average of seven attempts to break up before people in abusive relationships can get out mentally. They become as accustomed to the cycle of control as they are in love with their partner. The control their partner has exercised over their lives can make it difficult to consider living with it. One thing about control is that it takes the stress of making decisions out of your hands. When you're considering breaking up, suddenly, you're in control of making various life-changing decisions, and that brings stress with it. Often, it just feels easier to go back and try to make another go of it with your partner.

- **You share a life together**: You've built a life with this person and invested a great amount of energy into your shared dreams. Now you have to give all of that up, as well as your partner. That can be a tough pill to swallow, and many are often reluctant to give up what they've been building with their partner, even if he is abusive. However, the truth is that's another way your partner can manipulate and control you. Those dreams don't have to end just because your relationship does—you deserve to have a relationship where you can build your dreams in safety and with emotional support.

- **You're financially dependent**: Another reason many women choose to stay with an abusive partner is that they are financially dependent on their partner. You might believe you don't have enough money to take care of yourself. If you have been a homemaker for years, you might not have any work experience to get a job either. Additionally, if the two of you have children, the situation will be further complicated. It's not uncommon for a woman to stay at least until the children are out of the house.

- **Change is hard**: It can be frightening, financially difficult, and very uncomfortable to leave the life you built with someone else. For those who fear getting out of their comfort zone and completely changing their life, it can seem like an overwhelming challenge. There is a lot you will have to do to make this change, and the more intertwined your lives are, the more complicated getting out will be. It's something many abusive partners take advantage of; they seek to isolate you purposefully, so you won't have many options should you decide you want out.

These tactics that your partner uses to exert power and control over you are not love. Love is safe, supportive, trusting, and respectful, and if your partner is treating you in any other way, that's not love. You deserve love, and you deserve a life free from abuse. That's easy to say, but even our culture can make it difficult. Aside from your personal feelings about the situation, there are frequently societal pressures as well. That further complicates the matter. Let's look at a few of those.

Why She Stayed—Societal Pressures

Aside from the many personal reasons people have for staying in an abusive relationship, there are also a number of societal pressures. You might not like to think these pressures affect you as much as they do, but the fact is that they can exert a very strong influence on your decision to stay or leave. Here are some reasons why society can affect your decision.

- **Society normalizes unhealthy behavior**: There are many examples of society normalizing abusive behaviors. These behaviors might be seen regularly on television, in the movies, or through other social media forums. If you are constantly exposed to images of men exercising control over their female partners, you can come to see that as normal. That doesn't mean you see it as healthy, but you see it as a kind of normal behavior. When you believe the abusive treatment to which you are subjected is normal, you may not even realize you're in an abusive relationship.

- **Society perpetuates the belief that you shouldn't give up**: It's not uncommon to see pop culture glamorizing the idea that you shouldn't give up on someone—that if you just stick it out or forgive and forget, everything will work out. This makes it seem like if you leave, you're basically a quitter. This can put enormous pressure on a person in an abusive relationship to stay way longer than they should just to prove that they gave it their all. The truth is that being loyal is great, but a real friend or lover should never want to hurt or put you in danger. The emotional or physical abuse you might be experiencing is *not* love, and you should *never* feel pressured into staying in a relationship where you're being treated poorly.

- **Social pressure to be in a perfect relationship**: There is a great deal of pressure to be in the perfect relationship, and our modern age of social media only accentuates that pressure. The truth is that you likely thought you were getting into the perfect relationship when it was just getting started. I know I did. So, you might have told all your family and friends about just how wonderful he is, and to think you might now have to go back and tell everyone that he is not what he appeared to be at first can cause a lot of stress. The truth is there is no way you could have known he wasn't what he seemed. He hid his true self from you. How could you possibly have known? Your true friends and family will understand that, and they should support you in your decision to leave.

- **Fear of being judged**: It's easy to feel embarrassed to admit that your partner has been abusive to you. You don't want to be pitied or look down on, or even marginalized for failing at your relationship. That can keep many people from admitting they're in an abusive relationship, but the truth is that, once again, your true friends and family will support you and want you to get out, so you can be happy and find a partner who will truly be your perfect love.

When you understand that there are not only your personal feelings about breaking up with your partner that affect your decision, but there are also a whole host of societal pressures that work to keep you together as well, it's no wonder you're having difficulty. The reasons behind why society often takes an active role in pressuring you to stay in your relationship lies in our not-so-distant past. For much of human history, communities and families have had a vested interest in seeing that couples stay together. It worked to further their own agenda of community growth and increased influence. Families want the relationship to work out so there can be stability as the family grows and undergoes various changes. In the past, stability guaranteed consistent access to resources necessary for survival; thus, changes like breaking up with your partner were discouraged, and in some cases, illegal. These pressures are not gone just because we've entered a more modern age. Although the survival of a relationship is no longer tied as closely to community and family stability and health, that kind of thinking has been ingrained in our brains. And, your brain is a big factor in why it hurts so much to break up.

And Then, There's Your Brain

We all know how much breakups suck. If you're like I was, you don't even want to get out of bed, let alone talk to anyone or even eat. In fact, it can feel as though you don't have the physical strength to do those things. You just lay in bed, staring at the walls, stuck in your thoughts, and crying your eyes out. Sadness, anxiety, and anger are all your constant companions. People are telling you that you'll feel better, but even if you really do believe them while stuck in grief, it can feel like you're dying. That's not just descriptive hyperbole; there's a physical reason why it feels like that, and it has to do with how your brain processes a break up.

First, a little history on why your brain is programmed like this. Back when our species was evolving into the dominant species we are today, we needed company to survive. Humans are not fast—they can't outrun predators or prey, they are not strong compared to other animals, and they are woefully lacking in defense mechanisms—they also don't possess sharp fangs and or long claws.

The one thing humans do have, however, is our large brains and strength in numbers. Before we had certain modern technologies, however, we only had our strength in numbers to help us survive the very real dangers of wild animals that could eat us. If we did something in our community to get thrown out, it could all mean certain death. That possibility was so likely, in fact, that it is the reason we may fear things like speaking in public more than death itself. If we speak in public and say something wrong, we could get ostracized, and that, in the past, could easily mean our death. Nowadays, of course, you can be ostracized from one community and just take up with another. So, survival isn't as big of a deal, but the problem is that our brains have not had a chance to catch up to that reality. The human brain still reacts as it has for so many millennia to the possibility of being ostracized.

A break up is like being ostracized. You're being separated from your family group, and in the past, that was a dangerous situation. So, your brain responds as if it is still very dangerous. In fact, the brain processes a breakup just like it processes physical pain. Studies using brain scanners to film the activity in various parts of the brain have found that when you break up with someone, the same parts of the brain—the insula and anterior cingulate, to be specific—light up with activity when people experience physical pain when burnt.

This is also shown by how the brain releases natural painkillers—opioids—when you've been rejected by potential suitors. Participants in one study were shown pictures of imaginary people they were told were on a dating website, and they were then asked which ones they liked. After identifying the ones they liked, they were later told that their feelings weren't returned. In other words, they were told they were rejected by the people they indicated they would like. After being told that, their brains released opioids to kill the pain. This happened, even though the people in the study knew they were not really being rejected and the people were imaginary. Still, their body responded as if it was a real rejection.

That's powerful stuff, because it really means that your body treats even the slightest rejection like it is a potential threat to your survival; remember that, in the past, it was. It's understandable given our history why the brain would respond this way, and it also explains why a break up feels so bad. Now, no one wants to feel so terrible, and even though you now have some understanding about why you feel that way, it still doesn't make the pain that much easier to bear.

You might be wondering if you should have to go through the terrible feelings that come with a breakup, and unfortunately, the answer is yes. The reason is that avoiding the emotions is what traps them in your body, and that will result in prolonged suffering associated with PTSD. It can help, however, to understand the stages you go through as you grieve the loss of your relationship.

Grief Stages

Recognizing the stages of grief will help you go through with any loss, even that of an abusive relationship. Let's examine each stage.

Stage 1—Shock: Shock is the first stage that occurs when the breakup is fresh. This doesn't necessarily mean the kind of physical shock you experience with a physical injury; it is more of an emotional one. This happens even when you want to break up and are looking forward to it. It feels like the breakup doesn't really feel *real*. You still can't quite wrap your mind around it. That's what shock is like in this situation.

Stage 2—Denial: Denial can also take many forms, but it is essentially an inability to deal with the enormity of what has happened. You might believe that it just didn't happen or that your ex will come back somehow. You could also find that you have difficulty accepting the truth of the breakup during this stage.

Stage 3—Anger: This is listed as the third stage, but the truth is that it can happen at any time during the grief process. You've been living in a situation that has generated a lot of fear for a long time, but now, as that fear is subsiding, you'll start to feel real anger for what happened. You realize that you never deserved the treatment you endured, and you're outraged that they would do such a thing. How could they treat you or anyone that way? Use this phase to generate the energy you need to get yourself out or help you move on.

Stage 4—Bargaining: This stage can be particularly problematic. Because of the separation from someone you at least once loved, it's possible you'll start looking at the relationship through those rose-colored glasses again. You might start to bargain to regain what you feel you've lost. You might bargain with God or your ex to try to make another go at it. In fact, it's during this stage that most people do try to make another go. They assume it will be different, but of course, if their partner hasn't done anything to heal his own wounds, the abuse will resume.

Stage 5—Depression: This is when your sadness really takes hold. It doesn't necessarily mean you will be clinically depressed, but you will feel sad. You might experience changes in your appetite, cry a lot, and want to withdraw from the world. It can feel like a dark hole, an abyss, but it's actually a good sign. When you reach this stage, you're in the home stretch. You're getting better.

Stage 6—Initial acceptance: This might initially feel like surrender, but you're simply accepting the terms of the break up. You might still feel pain, but you can also see the relationship more clearly for what it was. You'll be able to accept both your role and the role of your partner in both the good and bad of the relationship.

Stage 7—Hope: This is the stage where you're finally feeling better and moving on. You might see a picture of your ex, and instead of feeling sad or angry, you simply won't feel very much anymore. You'll go out with your friends, and instead of merely tolerating the outing like before, you'll really start to enjoy yourself. You're letting go of the bad feelings and are ready to get your life going again.

It's important to realize that these stages aren't set in stone. Each individual may have a different experience, or the stages may occur in a different order. You may also go into and out of various stages repeatedly. You may get angry, then depressed, and then go back to anger again, for example. There's no one-size-fits-all for the grief process following a break up. Although it's not universal, it is a basic framework for what you can expect.

It's Common to Miss Him

As you go through the stages of grief, you need to know that it's common to miss your ex, even despite his toxic behavior. He likely has some good qualities, and you might be romanticizing those. It's also not uncommon for partners of toxic people to have made that person the center of their universe. Leaving that behind creates a hole in your world. You also might still be holding onto hope that he will change. Furthermore, you've had to spend your whole life to start anew, and that can make you a little misty-eyed for the past, particularly as the pain of his bad behaviors starts to fade. There's nothing wrong with these feelings; they are completely normal. Just don't let them convince you to give it another go without evidence of real change; unless he seeks help for his behavioral problems, that's not likely to happen.

Suicidal Thoughts

Such a huge disruption in your life in combination with low self-esteem, depression, and trauma suffered during the relationship can often lead to suicidal ideation. If you experience thoughts about ending your life, it's really important to seek some professional help so you can process those feelings. It's not a sign of weakness—what you went through was extremely traumatic and destructive to your sense of identity and self-esteem. It's a wonder everyone doesn't consider suicide after a situation like that. Getting help to cope with those feelings and ideas is imperative. The world won't be nearly as bright without you in it. If you're in deep, call a suicide hotline and talk to someone. You can remain anonymous on those; however, afterward, seek help from a professional to get you through the worst of it. You can also employ some of the following techniques to help you take care of yourself as you process the pain. These strategies will be helpful no matter your emotional state.

Reestablish Your Safe Zone with Strong Boundaries

To do this, you might need to take a number of actions. Begin by establishing strong boundaries for your ex so he doesn't come around trying to get back together. It might even be necessary to cut off ties altogether, and that will be helpful for you too. By being exposed to anything that reminds you of your ex, you're just making it harder for both of you. You want to find stability in every area of your life. That can look different to different people, but basically, it can help you give yourself some time to heal if possible and get back into your daily routines. I would strongly recommend blocking him altogether for at least the first month after you leave him. Go somewhere he can't find you and don't answer emails, phone calls, or social media messages. Don't look at old pictures of the two of you together, and don't get involved in anything you have in common. Give yourself some time to recover from what has happened, and then you can go on to reconnect with your life. If your ex is persistent or dangerous in any way, you might need to refrain from having any contact at all ever again, and you may even need to get a restraining order to keep him from contacting you if needed. If you have to contact him—as might be the case if you have children—then do so only through lawyers or written messages like emails, so you can have documentation of the contact in case something happens.

Reconnect with Loved Ones

One thing that's helpful to do is reconnect with your loved ones. You have to remember that when you break up with someone, you've lost a part of your identity. When you became serious about that relationship, you incorporated them into your sense of identity, and now that has been torn away. Reconnecting with loved ones can help remind you of how lovable you are, what good company you are, and why someone would want to be in a relationship with you. This not only makes you feel good psychologically, but it also causes your brain to release endorphins—some of your body's feel-good hormones—and that makes you feel good physically.

Write in Your Journal

As we've discussed in the exercises at the end of each chapter, writing in a journal is not just a good way to document what happened, but it also helps you process how you feel about it. It has positive effects during times of crisis like a breakup. You can start by just writing out how you feel today or how you feel when certain things happen. From there, you would just let your writing flow. Try to write for 20 minutes each morning, and be kind to yourself as you do. Give yourself some words of encouragement and a few compliments as you make progress. You'll be surprised at how a little writing can really make you feel better.

Be Kind to You

It will take some time to go through this process, so don't set yourself up for failure by setting rigid expectations for when you should feel better or start doing various things again. Let yourself grieve properly and fully process your feelings. Treat yourself like you would treat your best friend if she were going through the same thing. Be your own best friend. Accept any feelings that arise and give yourself sympathy. It's hard to go through a breakup.

Be Active

Exercise triggers the release of those feel-good hormones, endorphins, mentioned earlier. It also helps you work the stress out of your body. You can plan your exercise to coincide with the times of the day that are most difficult for you. For example, if you notice you feel worse in the morning, then maybe go for a walk when you first wake up. If you know you'll have trouble falling asleep, you can do some stretching exercises to relax your muscles, then follow that up with an activity for your mind, like a crossword or good book. Both will relax your body and get you ready for sleep.

Get Rid of Your Inner Critic

When you notice negative thoughts cropping up, you'll want to oust that criticism and replace it with some positive affirmations. It might sound hokey, but it actually trains your brain to respond positively instead of negatively. It's common for people who are fresh out of an abusive relationship to blame themselves. If this is you, you might call yourself names, list your shortcomings, or even obsess over rejections. This is like throwing salt in your wound. Your brain's survival response has already been triggered by the breakup, and this will activate that response even more. So, remember to be your own best friend and treat yourself accordingly. Replace negative criticism with positive thoughts immediately. When you think, "I'm so stupid," replace it with, "I'm really learning so much more about relationships and myself." You could even try writing a letter to yourself, as if you were writing your best friend who's suffering from a breakup. These ideas will help you feel better about yourself and the situation, and practicing those positive affirmations to replace your negative thoughts will teach your brain to look on the bright side.

Learn Self-Soothing Techniques

Self-soothing techniques are things you can do to help yourself relax. There are a number of great techniques you can use, but here are a few that work well:

1. **Breathing exercises**: When you practice deep breathing that expands your stomach, you activate the vagus nerve. The vagus nerve is like the on/off switch for your parasympathetic nervous system. You might remember that it's the chill and relax nervous system. By stimulating that, you can overcome any anxiety that might arise. Try sitting in a comfortable position and closing your eyes. Bring your focus to your breathing and take ten deep breaths that expand your stomach. Just relax as you do this, and you'll find yourself feeling better when you're ready to get going again.

2. **Muscle relaxation**: This is a great technique to do right before bed, particularly if you have trouble sleeping. As you lay on the bed, close your eyes and mentally survey your body. Take ten deep breaths, then beginning at the top of your head, consciously focus on relaxing the muscles of each body part. Begin

with the muscles on your face and head, then progress to your neck, shoulders, arms and chest, belly, and then down to your hips, legs, and feet. Focus on each area and practice total relaxation. You might even fall asleep before you're done.

3. **Meditation**: Meditation has proven scientific effects on your physical and mental health. By meditating in the morning and every evening before going to bed, you help calm your mind, gain valuable insights into your experiences and personality, and help heal old wounds. It can lower your blood pressure, help you sleep, and calm anxiety. It's great any time you feel anxious or afraid. It also helps keep you grounded in the present so you can experience life more fully.

Reconnect with Ordinary Life

You might find it difficult to remember what life was like before your abusive relationship. You might believe that you're closed off from the world, and it might even be hard to trust people again. You might even have been isolated from your family and friends by your abusive partner. If that's the case, you might think you have no one to turn to, but you'll be surprised at how quickly people will rally to help you. You are not alone, and you're not the first person to go through this. Believe in your family and friends, and you'll find that they want to help you get over what you've experienced.

To Date or Not to Date

We'll talk more about building healthy, new relationships in subsequent chapters, but for our purposes here, suffice it to say that rebound relationships can actually be *helpful* during this phase. Although many psychologists may say that you shouldn't become involved with someone else for fear you might just trade one abuser for another, according to at least one study, starting a new relationship can still help build self-esteem and increase a sense of well-being. In fact, the people who had rebound relationships in this study were both more likely to detach from their ex quicker and feel more desirable and certain of themselves than those who didn't engage in such a relationship. Though you might not want to go right out and find a rebound relationship, you should still surround yourself with people in your life who make you feel good, fun, and worthwhile. These people will improve your self-esteem and help you pass the time until you can naturally start feeling better.

Make no mistake about it—getting out of any relationship, including an abusive one, is one of the most difficult things you'll ever do in your life. The effects you suffer from the abuse can linger for a long time and include depression, guilt, anger, anxiety, insomnia, emotional numbness, being easily frightened, avoidance of triggers, and difficulty maintaining relationships. Moreover, there is not one way to feel better or heal after leaving an abusive partner. What works for one person may not be very helpful for you. You may have to try several different tactics to help you heal. It also wouldn't be uncommon that you would try to reconcile with your ex after doubting your decision to leave him in the first place.

Even though the recovery process will be difficult, you need to remember how brave you were for taking that initial step of leaving in the first place. That took a great deal of strength, and now it is time to channel that strength into your healing, so you can get back on track to your happy and healthy life. You deserve happiness, and you also deserve to feel safe and worthwhile. So, let yourself go through the healing process. You will experience some difficult emotions, but let those emotions help you grow. Remember that every day that you no longer have to put up with abuse is another little piece of yourself that you recover. Eventually, those pieces will all fit together to reveal the new, better, and stronger you.

Mindfulness Exercise

This exercise will help you increase your body awareness regarding where you hold your grief. It's a mindfulness exercise that will help you be more aware of your body.

- Begin by sitting in a comfortable position, but one in which you will stay alert.

- Focus first on your breathing, and take ten deep, belly-expanding breaths.

- Next, create a safe place where you can go if you begin to experience too much stress. This could be somewhere like a quiet place in nature—the beach or a secluded forest—or a home where you always feel safe. Wherever your safe place is located, envision it and let the feeling of safety permeate your body.

- Now, think about your feelings about losing your relationship. Perhaps you're afraid that you won't get your life together or you'll never have another relationship. Let yourself feel that fear and let it play out. What happens if you can't get your life together? What if you lose your job or can't find one, or you lose your house and become homeless? What are the consequences of your fear?

- In the midst of experiencing these feelings—which you can escape from to your safe place at any time—notice what is happening in your body. Do you feel pain or tightness somewhere? Do you feel a heavy weight on your shoulders? Do you have a stomach or a headache? Where is the feeling in your body?

- Now, breathe into that part of your body. Really take expansive breaths into where you feel discomfort.

- Next, check the validity of your fear. Is it true that you're homeless? Maybe you're living in a shelter because of the abuse you've suffered, but is it true that you won't be able to get back on your feet? Most of the time, our fears are just that—fear. Think of all the reasons that your fears won't come true. For example, perhaps you have family or friends who will give you a place to stay. You're not addicted to any substances, and you're motivated to find work, so how likely is it that you won't be able to? It's probably not very likely under those circumstances. Go through this process while you're breathing deeply into the parts of your body that feel tight because of the fear.

- Finally, bring yourself back to a place of safety. Replace your negative fears with positive affirmations. If you fear losing your home, affirm something like, "I am experiencing expansive abundance in all areas of my life," and, "I have everything I need to live my best life." When you train your brain to think positively, you also train it to look for positive solutions to any problems you have. So, begin the affirmation process.

- When you have finished repeating your positive affirmations three times each, bring your focus back to your breath and take 10 to 20 more expansive breaths as you express gratitude for the things you have right now in your life. Begin with gratitude that you're not being exposed to abusive treatment anymore. If you're in a woman's shelter, express gratitude for such places and the people who understand what you're going through. If you're staying with family and friends, express gratitude for having them in your life.

- When you're ready, open your eyes.

When you finish this mindfulness exercise, it's time to journal what you experienced. The main goal of this exercise was to identify the areas of your body where you hold your emotions. For me, it was a tightness in my chest, but for you, it might be an upset stomach or aching head. You'll want to identify these areas because as you work the trauma out of your body, you'll need a high level of awareness to let it go.

Chapter Five: Changing Your Mindset—Preparing for PTSD Recovery

Step 5: Don't look back—move toward a new, psychopath-free life

Now that you've made the decision to leave your abusive partner, it's time to prepare for the healing process, so you can recover from the post-traumatic stress that caused many problems for you. The first step in doing this is to prepare your mind for a healthy recovery and new life. Part of the problem with the way many people view relationships is that we've been sold a bill of goods about what constitutes the perfect relationship. We've been told since we were young that Prince Charming would arrive, and we would know that it was right. Moreover, popular culture would have us believe there is only one right partner per customer—one true soulmate, one Mr. Right.

Of Fairy Tales and Pixie Dust

Our ideas about relationships are based on fairy tales, though the truth is a lot more complicated. You thought you had met Mr. Right—I know I did—but then he started to abuse you emotionally and maybe physically too. Why, Prince Charming wouldn't do that! You felt like he was your true soulmate, but now you have made the choice to leave him. Does that mean you'll never have another crack at it?

The truth is that there are a lot of Mr. Rights out there. There is no one true soulmate; there are instead many possible true loves. True love is a combination of respect, kindness, support, attraction, and, well, love. If those elements are not all present, you won't feel loved, and what's more, you won't *be* loved. The sad truth is that many people have been so badly abused as children that they don't know how to love. Although that is a tragedy, you can't help them by giving them real love. They have to choose to heal those wounds themselves to even be able to receive your love. And, what they are capable of giving you will only be an expression of their desire to exercise control over something in their lives. That's not love.

If you've been in a relationship with just such a person, your love, no matter how true, will be unable to heal them. Nothing external can heal them at that point. Their healing has to come from within. That's the first fairy tale to lay to rest. You won't be able to kiss the sleeping prince and bring him back to life; only he can wake himself up if he chooses to do so.

Another fairy tale that you'll need to let go of is that you only get one true love per customer. You'll love a lot of people in your life in many different ways. You thought your love for your abuser was true, and it likely was, but that doesn't mean you can't love someone else in the same way. There is no limit to the love that exists in the world, and there is no limit to the love you can choose to give. You might even go on loving your abuser after you've left him, but you must love yourself equally as much as you love him or anyone else, or your love cannot last. The most important relationship in your life is the one you have with yourself. If that's not in good shape, you won't be able to give anyone else true love. So, you have to commit to healing your wounds and learning to love yourself truly, just as you would your Prince Charming. Without self-love—genuine self-love—there can be no true love for anyone else in your life.

You might be thinking he was your soulmate, and you might think you'll never feel that strongly for anyone else. The truth is that the right person always enters your life at exactly the right time, making each and every individual who comes to you a kind of soulmate. Really, a soulmate is nothing more than a teacher—someone who brings you a life lesson. Your abuser brought you one kind of lesson, and it should spur you on to heal your wounds and seek self-love. Once you can do that, you'll find you're ready for the next soulmate teacher to arrive in your life. When you accept that everyone who comes to you in one form or another is here for your personal growth, you'll begin to look for the opportunities they bring you. You'll see the positive side of any relationship you have, and you'll understand that *all* of these people are soulmates.

Changing Your Mindset

Part of changing your mindset is letting go of the fairy tales we've been told, but another part is developing a positive mindset as you start moving forward. Every time you break up with someone, you come away with bruised emotions and lower self-esteem. You can come to doubt whether you're worthy of love or that you'll be able to find it again. One key is to remember that one story's ending is just another story's beginning. Life is, as Aerosmith likes to sing, a journey, not a destination. Your emotionally abusive relationship was just one part of your journey. It's time to let that leg of the journey fade into the past and become excited about this new beginning. Here are a few tips that can help you change your mindset to a positive one that anticipates the adventures to come.

Some Things Can't Be Fixed

Not every story on your journey will end like you want it to, but it will end exactly as it should. You might struggle with thoughts that you could have somehow fixed your relationship if you only would have said this or done that. The reality is, however, that some relationships simply won't have a happy ending, and that's okay. The problems we confront in life and the difficult times we endure are there to stimulate our continued growth. That's not just true for you; it's true for your abusive ex as well. Perhaps the experience of losing you will cause him to finally seek the help he needs. Maybe the loss will drive him into the arms of another who will help him find what he needs in life. Or maybe he will find someone else, and his cycle will never change. You can't know why things ended the way they did, but you can trust that the lessons you're receiving as a result of the experience will help you grow into a better person. Allow yourself to learn the lessons, so you won't repeat your mistakes. When you do that, you can move further down the path of your journey of life.

No One Loses Love

It is never wrong to love someone, and true love means loving them, even if they don't—or can't—love you back. You didn't do anything wrong when you fell in love with him, and it's not wrong if you still love him. However, you must love yourself as well, and that means you have to keep yourself safe from harm, both physically and mentally. That means you have to take necessary actions to avoid future harm by getting away from the source of abuse. He'll find his own way to wherever he is meant to go next. You will as well, so take the opportunity to channel that love you felt for him toward yourself. Love has a way of coming back to you when you give it freely, and it will always soften and purify your heart.

There is No Mr. Wrong

Even though this relationship did not work out, it taught you something about yourself and the world around you. It's helping you grow into a stronger person, and it's teaching you how to improve the relationship you have with yourself going forward. That's not a failure; that's a huge success. Without this relationship, you might never have learned what you needed to learn to be ready for your next Mr. Right. Remember that within every challenge in life is the opportunity to become a better version of yourself. How would you know what you want out of a relationship if you didn't experience things you didn't want? There is no Mr. Wrong; he's just another teacher who helped you learn about yourself.

Let Go of Expectations

All of the experiences you have in your life help define you, so when life doesn't go as you planned, let it go and move toward what your life is becoming. You need to seize the opportunities for growth, but to do that, you have let go of what is lost. Let yourself move beyond the negative feelings and experience of your abusive relationship because something better is waiting as you open up to the new possibilities in your life. Don't forget the past, but learn from it as you move into your new future.

Take Control of Your Own Life

You don't have control over your ex partner, but without him, you now have control over your life. Take it, so that you can move toward your dreams for your own life. You have a great opportunity to take your life in the direction you want it to go. This will allow you to live life fully as you achieve your own goals. You no longer have to live in accordance with someone else's goals; it's your time now to move in the direction of your ideal life. Don't waste another minute on what might have been. Look toward what can be *now*.

How Do You Change Your Mindset?

As you move into the process of healing from the trauma you've experienced, the power of positive thinking can help with both physical and mental benefits. Those benefits have been supported through various scientific studies. They include improving your self-confidence, boosting your mood, and reducing your risk of hypertension, depression, and other stress-related problems. That sounds great, but what does it really mean, and how do you make the change?

First, let's define what we mean by *positive thinking*. This involves positive imagery or visualization and increasing positive self-talk to promote general optimism. So, how can you do this exactly? Let's look at some great ideas to get you started.

Begin the Day with Positivity

How your day begins can set the tone for the entire day, so you want it to begin with something positive. The best way to do that is to start each day with a positive affirmation or even a list of positive affirmations. You could create several positive affirmations to repeat each morning. You can do this before you get out of bed, or you can tape these positive affirmations to your mirror and let them be the first things you see each morning. Some examples include the following:

- Today, I am experiencing all that is good and taking steps toward achieving my goals.
- I will be at my best today.
- I am seizing all opportunities that come my way.
- I am learning to be my best today.
- I am improving each day.

Try it for a week and see just how much your mood improves, as will your performance.

Focus on the Good

Everyone faces obstacles, and there's no such thing as a perfect day, but if you encounter a challenge, focusing on the benefits, even the small ones, can brighten your day. Try this when anything difficult happens—finish this sentence about any challenges or obstacles: "It's good because..." For example, if you're stuck in a traffic jam, "It's good because now I can listen to my favorite radio station." If you have a difficult day at work, "It's because I'm learning something new." There's a reason that each challenge you face is good in some way, however small. Seek those reasons out, and you train your brain to look for advantages in every situation. Doing this repeatedly will make the behavior a habit.

Laugh, Even When Things are Difficult

Sometimes, all you can do is laugh, but when you do, you'll find you feel a lot better about almost any trying situation. These challenges always make for good stories later on, so try to find something humorous to add to the tale. For example, if you lose your job, what's the most absurd or ridiculous job you could look for next? Make a joke out of it by saying something like, "Well, now that I don't work at the brokerage anymore, I think I might like to try my hand at bubblegum sculpting." Now, let yourself imagine your life as a bubblegum sculptor; it should make you laugh and help you feel better. It will make you a more interesting, creative, and imaginative person too.

Look for Opportunities in Everything

No matter what happens, there is always an opportunity present in each and every failure. If you made a mistake, learn from it. Consider your abusive relationship, for example—what did you learn? What were the signs in the beginning? What were the red flags you overlooked because you couldn't believe it was happening? Conceptualize how you might handle the situation differently if something similar happens in the future. For example, you might make an excuse for your ex the first time he insulted you, so how would you handle it with a new man? You could decide that you would immediately tell him you won't accept that kind of treatment, and if it happens again, you will leave. Or, you could decide to leave right away. Whatever way you would choose to handle it going forward, write down three new rules to follow.

Turn the Negative Into Positive

We've talked about noticing your negative self-talk and turning it positive, but let's go into a little more depth about just how to do that. First, it can help if you carry a notebook around for about a week to document just the negative self-talk. Each time you catch yourself thinking something negative, stop and document what happened. Where were you? Were you with someone, and if so, who? What were the circumstances that led up to the negativity? What were you feeling at the time? Let's say, for example, that you're reminiscing about some of the good times you had with your ex, and you start to think about how stupid you were to let him go. So, you would document that you were reminiscing, and if there was someone there, note who it was and what they had to say in the exchange. You would also note your feelings at the time. Were you sad? Bittersweet? You could also write down exactly what the negative thought was; in this example, it might be, "I'm so stupid for letting him go."

The next step in this process is to challenge the negative belief. Is it true? Were you stupid, or was it self-preservation? Having experienced this myself, I can confirm it was not stupid. You were doing what you had to do to get out of an abusive situation, and in fact, leaving was both courageous and intelligent. So, that thought is not accurate, but why did you think so? Could it be that you are holding some core beliefs about yourself that you learned as a child? Did someone tell you at some point in your life that you were being stupid? Perhaps it was even in a situation where you were standing up for yourself and should have been praised instead of insulted. Take some time to remember the moment. What were the circumstances? Who told you that you were being stupid? What was their situation? Maybe they didn't know any better, or perhaps they never had the proper training to deal well with children. Can you feel compassion for them? Can you feel compassion for the little you who felt so bad about herself? Can you give that little you the compassionate, loving, and positive response you should have received? Give yourself the love you deserve, and you'll never allow anyone else to treat you badly again.

Once you've fully explored the reasons behind the negative statement, write down a positive alternative. For the thought, "I'm so stupid for letting him go," you could instead think, "I'm learning to love myself and give myself respect." Go through this process for every negative thought you experienced over the week you were observing yourself. Now, carry your list of positive alternatives with you, and each time you think something negative, refer to that list for a positive alternative. Speak it out loud, and then reaffirm it twice more. Again, this trains your brain to react positively out of habit rather than negatively, which has probably been your habit up until this point. It takes an average of 28 days to replace a bad habit with a good one, so stick with it until thinking positively becomes your go-to response.

Stay Present

Stay in the present, and you'll find that even the worst moments change and pass far more quickly than you think. Are you feeling down? Stay present and sit with the feeling. You'll find that it's not constant. It changes, and before long, you'll be feeling better. You'll also see that most bad moments are not as bad as you might initially think, and you'll also discover that you're stronger than you might think too. Additionally, most often when you're thinking about something bad, it's because you are remembering a past event, such as might be the case with your ex; in other cases, you may be looking to the future. In other words, you're *not* in the present. Your ex isn't mistreating you in the present, so if you're lamenting on something he said, you're actually in the past. Stay in the present and feel the emotions you're really having. You might, for example, be feeling lonely, and that is causing you to think back on a time when you had someone in your life. But let yourself sit with the loneliness, and you'll find that the emotion changes quickly. You'll also find that you can be more creative with problem-solving. You're lonely right now, so maybe you can go talk to your neighbor or call up a good friend. Before you know it, you won't be feeling so lonely anymore.

Surround Yourself with Positive People

When you've ended your relationship, it's also a good time to clean the house of the people who really aren't positive influences in your life. You don't have to confront them actively, but you can choose not to be around them anymore. Instead, surround yourself with positive people who really have your best interests at heart. These are the people who will encourage you to take steps necessary to heal yourself and reach your goals for your best life. They will offer you positive, constructive advice on how to move forward, will be there for you, and will be there when you need a friend to talk to. Your true friends will help you through the sadness and encourage you to reach for the stars.

These positivity tips can help you overcome your self-doubt and fear as you recover from the trauma to which you've been exposed. What's more, by changing your mindset to one that is positive, it provides compounding returns and huge benefits. You deserve to have people in your life who respect and treat you with kindness and compassion. You've experienced what it's like to have someone who's not kind in your life, and you've learned from that experience. Now it's time to apply what you've learned and gather positive, encouraging, and loving people to your circle, so they can help you become the best version of yourself.

Mindset Exercise

Now is the time for you to reflect on the lessons you've learned from your experience. What did you learn about yourself through this experience? Write down three things you didn't know about yourself that you know now and reflect on how they make you feel. If you feel bad about something you learned, write down what you can do the next time such a situation arises. What can you do that will make you feel better about yourself? Resolve to make that change.

Next, provide some insight into the red flags you chose to ignore about your relationship. In hindsight, what behaviors bothered you, but you made excuses for your instead of addressing? List at least five, and along with those, make some new rules about what you would do if you are confronted with that behavior in the future.

Next, follow the advice for changing your negative thinking into positive affirmations. Carry a notebook around with you and make note of each time you think something negative about yourself. Explore the origins of those negative thoughts and produce a list of positive alternatives. Record everything in your journal while allowing yourself to write freely about the feelings this experience generated about yourself, your past, and how it affected your present.

Two Letters to Your Ex

The next step to changing your mindset is to place the past firmly behind you. You'll do this by writing two letters to your ex. Let's look at each letter.

1. **Letter #1**: The goal of this letter is to let go of the pain. In this letter, you will write to your ex all about the sadness, other negative emotions, broken dreams, disappointment, blame, and pain you endured during your relationship. Don't hold anything back; let him know all about the pain he caused you. You can set your alarm for 15 minutes while you write, but feel free to write longer if it takes more time. The key is to let it all out. Tell him how much he hurt you, how he destroyed your life together, and how angry and sad you are because of it. Really pour out your soul to him. Release every negative emotion he caused you in this letter. Let yourself cry while you're doing this or yell if that's what you need to do, but get every negative emotion out of your body. Once you're happy with your letter, read through it one more time, then burn it safely. The pain is in your past now.

2. **Letter #2**: Wait a few days before writing this second letter. This is a letter of gratitude to your ex. In this letter, you'll recall all of the good times you had together, positive moments, gifts, fun you had together, and dreams you built with each other. Maybe you had wonderful children together or took that dream vacation with one another. Maybe you're even grateful for the painful life lesson he gave you, since it has helped you grow and made you stronger. Again, set your alarm clock for 15 minutes, but feel free to write longer if you need to. Recall every single good thing that you had together. When the letter is ready, read through it again and allow yourself to feel the gratitude fully. Let it spread throughout your body lovingly. After reading through it, burn this letter as well. Now, everything about that relationship is in the past.

Chapter Six: How Can I Start Over Again? First Steps Toward Recovering from C-PTSD Caused by a Toxic Relationship

Step 6: The way back home

The first step towards recovery from C-PTSD includes education. It's important to understand the roles that each person plays in relationship transactions. One of the first things you want to understand is the roles we play in our relationships, specifically as it relates to drama. A good model for this is the Karpman Drama Triangle.

As you can see from the illustration above, there are three roles in the drama triangle—this is the triangle at the top of the image. These roles can shift, and they reflect both personal responsibility and power roles that emerge in a conflict situation. The three roles defined are the following:

- **The Victim**: When you assume the role of the victim, you feel oppressed, victimized, helpless, hopeless, and powerless. You also feel as though you cannot make decisions, solve problems, gain insight, or have pleasure in life. If you are in a victim role, you will actually seek out a persecutor and a rescuer, even when you're not being victimized.

- **The Rescuer**: The rescuer is a classic enabler. This means they feel guilty if they don't rescue people who need it, but their attempts to rescue have negative effects. They basically give the victim permission to fail. For the rescuer, the reward they receive is that they are no longer the focus of attention in their own mind. They don't have to think about their own anxiety and problems because they are focused instead on rescuing someone. Their reason behind rescuing others, therefore, is to avoid their own problems.

- **The Persecutor**: The persecutor is the villain in this drama. They are controlling, blaming, angry, oppressive, authoritarian, rigid, and superior-feeling individuals. They generate the fear that's at the heart of the drama triangle.

An interesting phenomenon occurs in the drama triangle: when one person takes on the role of either the victim or persecutor, the drama begins. The person who takes on either of these roles then enlists other players into the conflict. The rescuer is compelled to enter the situation. These roles, however, are dynamic and can shift. The victim, for example, might take on the role of persecutor and attack the rescuer.

This conflict situation persists because each participant, frequently unconsciously, plays their role in order to fulfill their own psychological needs and desires. In other words, they are all acting on their own selfish desires rather than for altruistic or genuinely responsible reasons. Between the persecutor and the victim, there is often a relationship based on codependency, and the rescuer can help keep the victim codependent by encouraging them as a victim. In this way, the victim gets their needs met because the rescuer is taking care of them.

The rescuer gets certain benefits that aren't always as clear, but they involve egoistic boosts and/or a distraction from their own problems. And, of course, the persecutor is acting in the way they do entirely to satisfy their own needs. These roles become habitual, so each person automatically assumes their role when a conflict arises. Additionally, each player in this little drama learns their roles in their childhood family. If you are a victim now, you were likely a victim in your family growing up. If you are a rescuer, you were probably a hero kid in your childhood. That doesn't mean you can't change roles, but it's the role of choice when conflicts arise. This is why part of the recovery process for C-PTSD lies in understanding the origins of your role.

Victim Syndrome

This is the first step to healing: education. If you don't understand what happened and why, you might be doomed to repeat your role as victim again and again. There's even a name for it and that is victim syndrome. People who suffer from victim syndrome are always complaining about the bad things that seem to be constantly happening to them. They believe they have no control over their lives and feel no sense of responsibility for the things that happen. They frequently display passive-aggressive behaviors and can quickly morph into victimizers who attack those who would try to help them. Their behavior is self-defeating and can become masochistic.

Frequently, victim syndrome results from childhood trauma. Someone with this problem may have been a victim of abuse as a child or witnessed abuse, perhaps between their parents. Abuse between or from parents can affect a child profoundly, since those are their earliest models of the opposite sex. An abused child might pity the abused parent and end up falling into the same trap. They could learn to model the behaviors, for example, of a mother who was always sacrificing her needs for everyone else in her family, or who constantly gave up her own dreams to support those of her husband. On the other hand, that same child might decide that to avoid becoming a victim of abuse, they must become like the abusive parent. This is how the cycle of abuse is passed on from generation to generation.

For women with a psychopathic father—or even just a cold, unavailable father—they frequently are attracted to narcissistic or psychopathic men. It's a way for them to work through the issues they had with their first image of men, i.e., their father. They are, in essence, trying to relive that relationship with an abusive partner, but this time they are certain they will make it work out. The cold, distant, narcissistic man she loves will suddenly realize how much he loves her and change his ways—if only she behaves appropriately. The problem is that even if that were to happen—something highly unlikely in the case of a narcissist or psychopath—it wouldn't fix the problem. It's an inside job. You have to fix it from the inside, and when you do, you will stop looking for external solutions. Until that time, you will likely keep making poor choices in your relationships.

It's also possible that someone suffering from a victim mentality can develop a martyr complex. This person comes to desire the feeling of repeated victimization. In a sense, it's the devil they know, so it's where they feel most comfortable. If you suffer from this, you might even seek out your own victimization by placing yourself in relationships that will cause suffering. This is also associated with an inner masochism, where you may come to see yourself as deserving of this treatment. You might even reject offers of help from other people. Of course, this is a wholly unsatisfying way to live, but how can you change it? How do you stop being a victim?

Ending Your Victim Mentality

There are a number of things you can do to break out of the victim role. It's important to explore the underlying reasons for your victim mentality with a qualified therapist, but beyond that, here are a few practical tips that can help as well.

- **Take responsibility for your needs and desires.** To do this, you must first determine what you want and what you consider important. Make a list of your values and desires, then determine what you need to do to make those things happen, for yourself. Don't look to someone else to supply you with what you need. Don't blame anyone for obstacles that arise or wait for anyone to help you get what you want; just start doing it for yourself.

- **Practice saying no.** One tactic that many persecutors use is preying on your inability to say no when asked to do something. If you don't want to do something, don't do it. You have needs and preferences, just like everyone else. It's only you who can agree to do something, and it's also only you who can say no. Saying no means taking responsibility for your happiness and sense of integrity.

- **Don't blame others.** You are the one responsible for your actions and how your life turns out. If you blame someone else for something that didn't turn out well for you, you're saying they are responsible for your happiness and life. That's simply not true. This is related to learning to say no, of course, as well as taking responsibility for your own actions and results.

- **Practice gratitude.** Practice gratitude for all the wonderful things you have in your life. Don't put all your focus on areas of lack. Instead, focus on the abundance you have, and that will draw more abundance into your life.

- **Make a list of how you can change bad situations**. If you're in a bad situation, no matter how you got there, make a list of ways you can change it. What can you do to improve the situation or get out of it? There is always something, and by focusing on what you have the power to do, you'll find a way to change your circumstances. Even for someone in a dire situation like prison, if they choose to focus on educating themselves in preparation for their release, not only will they be in a better place when they get out, but the change in their attitude will also have a ripple effect on those around them.

- **Practice forgiveness.** If you play the victim, you hold onto the bitterness and anger of having been wronged. That very act continues to victimize you. It poisons your experiences and keeps you stuck in place. Let go of your anger, forgive your persecutor, forgive yourself, and allow yourself to move on. Practice compassion for the person who has wronged you. My ex and others like him are suffering from a mental disorder, one that has deep roots of insecurity, so deep in fact that they are always needing to find the faults in other people to bolster their own self-esteem. Can you imagine what it's like inside their minds? The fearful thoughts they must constantly be feelings spurs their toxic behavior. That's sad, and I can have compassion for my ex. Can you have compassion for yours? This doesn't mean you would allow him to continue to mistreat you, but you can let go of the resentment you've been holding against him because you have compassion for him. This is forgiveness, and it really is critical for you to move forward.

- **Inside work**. This is where you have to go inside and give yourself the love and support that your distant, cold, narcissistic, or psychopathic father never gave you. You have to heal your inner child, and that means getting to the core of what you experienced that led to your victim mentality, and then becoming your own superhero. You have to save and give yourself what you never got from your distant parent. This typically involves some deeper level therapy, but when you can heal that fragile little you who just couldn't understand why your father didn't love you, you open up your heart and your life blossoms. You also stop looking for solutions in the men who are so similar to your father. Instead, you start building healthy relationships.

Now that you understand more clearly the drama triangle, the goal is to move from that dynamic to the dynamic seen in the power triangle, mirrored below the drama triangle. You want to go from victim to creator, and instead of persecutors and rescuers, you want to be surrounded by loving facilitators and mentors. You want your interactions to come from a place of love. To make that shift, you have to understand more about your emotions and responses to trauma.

Differentiating Between Mental and Physical Anxiety

One of the keys for trauma survivors is to understand interplay between physical and mental anxiety. What happens with C-PTSD is that your trauma causes your physical anxiety to build up to the point where your body's responses to trauma become the new enemy. In short, your biggest fear becomes fear itself.

Mental anxiety is easier to control with cognitive therapeutic methods, but physical anxiety requires different self-help methods to alleviate it. Although you may know in your mind that you're really not in any danger, your body might still react as if it is, and you will still then experience the reality of the body over that of the mind. For example, if you've been "trained" by your abuser to cower every time he criticizes you, your body might go through a similar reaction if a boss is giving you a performance review. Although there's a world of difference between your traumatic experience and a performance review, your body doesn't know that.

To help with this kind of problem, sensorimotor psychotherapists use mindfulness, empathy, and a loving presence to work on both cognitive understanding of what is happening and physical responses. Basically, they can help you integrate the two so both your body and mind are on the same page. This can help you gain a new understanding of power dynamics that are not traumatic in nature, and you will respond differently as a result.

Trauma Integration and Tuning into Emotions

Trauma integration really means being able to be honest with yourself and feel what you are feeling without becoming overwhelmed by it. You might, for example, be someone who intellectualizes your emotions rather than feeling them. However, if you don't allow yourself to feel them, they become trapped in your body and come out at inopportune times. You want to be able to sit down and have a dialogue with yourself to explore your emotions, so you can honestly feel them and let them go. This allows you to really understand your emotions and be with what is, rather than what you think should or could be.

To integrate your trauma and tune into your emotions properly, you will actually need to rewire your brain to increase your body and self-awareness. This will help you to tune into your emotions genuinely and heal your trauma. Let's look at some of the treatment approaches that can help you do this. Before we begin, it's important to note that safety is vital to the healing process. Trauma triggers alarm systems in our brains, leading hypervigilance and reactions that are common in someone facing imminent danger. Part of the healing process is to learn to feel safe in the world, around others, and in our own bodies. With that said, if you feel at all overwhelmed anytime you're working on a healing treatment, it's important to go to a safe place in your mind and stop what you're doing until you believe you can continue safely.

Trauma-Informed Treatments

Cognitive behavioral therapy is a great means to overcome some trauma, but it's not always the most helpful technique for those who have survived childhood trauma. So, if some of your issues around victimhood arose in your childhood, there are other types of therapies that might be more helpful for you. You might know that your beliefs are not rational, but you can't control the physical responses. That's because your irrational beliefs and physical responses are coming from your emotional brain, which is the part of your brain that responds in survival mode without really consulting your rational mind. To change that, you need to rewire your emotional brain. The following forms of therapy are recommended by trauma experts for doing just that.

1. Eye Movement Desensitization and Reprocessing (EMDR)

A lot of your traumatic memories are images, sensations, or feelings that have been split off from the original memory. EMDR works to reassemble that information into packages that can be understood more rationally. It does this by stimulating the brain using eye movements that help those memories feel less intense. It's related to rapid eye movement (REM), which has been shown to be associated with mood regulation.

In essence, the more REM sleep you get, the less depressed you feel. REM sleep is also associated with how memories change over time, as it dissects the importance of memories to you emotionally. In short, REM sleep helps you identify the associations between memory fragments, which helps you process the memory better. That's how EMDR works too: it "frees up" the trauma by moving it over to your regular memory as a reassembled unit. That allows you to put the traumatic experience into its broader context, which ultimately makes it appear more distant and allows you to see that it is part of your past rather than your present. This form of therapy has shown great success and can work very quickly too.

2. Somatic Experiencing (SE)

This was developed by Peter Levine and involves teaching patients simple albeit effective ways to mobilize their body's healing systems. A therapist trained in this technique can help you release frozen psychological states that overwhelm you. Several of the therapies we're discussing here are based on how that trauma becomes trapped in your body unless you take certain steps to release it. This is based on research that found that animals release trauma with physical trembling following an life-threatening incident. They can appear as though they are having a seizure, but then they suddenly get up and are fine. They also don't suffer from PTSD, so the theory goes that by allowing your body to release that trauma, it helps relieve your PTSD symptoms. These kinds of therapies have had great success.

SE involves tracking your sensations, feelings, imagery, and body movements as you work through traumatic memories. By allowing your body to move—to tremble, shudder, or even just move slowly like the animals' bodies—you release that stored trauma, which will make a huge difference in both your physical and mental responses to trauma triggers going forward.

3. Pesso Boyden System Psychomotor (PBSP)

This is a body-mind approach created by two professional dancers—Albert Pesso and Diane Boyden—who discovered that their students experienced psychological relief from traumatic memories, triggers, and responses when they expressed their emotions through movement. The technique involves learning several exercises that allow you to recognize both physical and emotional signals coming from your body more easily. In this way, you can articulate the meaning of the signals and help move the trauma out of your body as you do.

4. Comprehensive Resource Model (CRM)

This is a holistic approach that often works for people with severe dissociative disorders. This is where you would simply detach from your emotions when triggered. CRM therapy techniques can help teach you several empowering internal resources you can access and use in a concentric sequence to process the emotional stimulation. Basically, these internal resources help integrate issues that arise into a neurological "scaffolding" of those resources in your mid-brain, limbic system, and neocortex; within these three sections of your brain is where experiences are logged and interpreted. When these issues are integrated, you can then use specific breathing techniques, somatic embodiment skills, and neurological and spiritual resourcing to process the situation. This allows you to feel safe and highly conscious (as opposed to detached) while you process your trauma.

5. **Internal Family Systems Therapy (IFS)**

This therapy was developed when a family therapist, Richard Schwartz, noticed that several of his clients spoke about "parts of themselves." IFS therapy seeks to integrate those parts, or sub-personalities—into your core self, or the part of you that has remained undamaged, confident, and compassionate. Each part brings different resources you can use to process past and current trauma, so you can resolve your emotional issues. The focus is on harmonizing your internal family.

6. Tension, Stress, and Trauma Release (TRE)

This is another therapy based on the observation that animals and children shake when they're scared, thereby releasing the trauma from their body. Adults often suppress that urge, and the result is that the trauma is still stored in the body. By working with an experienced therapist, you can use these techniques to release that stored trauma. By going back through the memory and allowing your body to shake, it calms the nervous system and releases muscle tension caused by the stored trauma. You should work with a skilled therapist, however, because if this therapy is done too much and/or too soon, it can feel as though you're being re-traumatized.

Movement and Breathing-Based Therapies

Another type of healing involves using movement, breathing, and meditation to heal complex PTSD. Techniques such as yoga, Tai Chi, Qi Gong, and Taekwondo can help you process your trauma by increasing mindfulness. They can help you notice muscle tension and relieve that through relaxation techniques. They can train you to notice your breathing patterns and change those to help reduce stress. They help you become more aware of your body and what it needs, and teach you to approach your body's reaction with curiosity rather than fear. This helps you feel safe in your own body.

Participants who trained in these techniques reported improved relaxation response skills, such as slowing their breathing and heart rates when stressed. They also came to realize that discomfort is not a permanent condition, which was an understanding that helped those negative feelings subside. They also noticed more the connections between their emotions and their bodies. When you become aware of where you hold emotional tension, you can focus on movements to release those feelings. All of this builds self-esteem and contributes profoundly to healing trauma.

Healing Through Human Connection— Relational Healing

These techniques focus on helping you heal your trauma in the context of your relationships with other people. Alcoholic Anonymous is one example of a group that uses this kind of healing. Basically, your healthy relationships provide a place of both physical and emotional safety where you can discuss and process your trauma openly. This is not a situation where you can heal within the context of your toxic relationship; rather, a quality relationship is required to develop trust for relational healing.

That means it must be a relationship where empathy is expressed, so you can feel heard and understood. It also must feel safe enough for you to demonstrate authentic vulnerability. You need to be able to discuss your experience without fear of judgment. You also need to be able to both speak about your experiences and listen to others, and you must work collaboratively to repair the damage done. This kind of healing will help you see that there are others like you who have suffered similar traumas. That, in and of itself, can be very healing.

These techniques often involve mentors who have gone through something similar and can help you when you're feeling particularly overwhelmed by emotions you can't seem to control. They can also involve people who see the best in you and are willing to help you find it for yourself. These people are referred to as *true others*, and they can help you reflect back the best they see in you, so you can see it too.

Another type of relational healing involves imagined nurturing. If you didn't receive the kind of nurturing that helps develop secure attachments in adulthood—a common reason for becoming attracted to toxic people—you can heal that through either real face-to-face connections or by using your imagination. Both real and imagined connections have the same effect on the brain. An example of this kind of experience is the inner child journey, which uses both face-to-face contact and visualization to experience childhood trauma, but it gives it a different outcome. You would provide your inner child with the nurturing she should have received but didn't. You become, in essence, your own hero and your own excellent parent, and you remain that way for your inner child into adulthood. This helps you break the bonds of old trauma that may be responsible for your adult attraction to toxic relationships.

All of these techniques can help you begin rewiring your brain to heal old trauma, whether that be from a more recent experience or childhood experiences that damaged your adult self-image. What works best for you will depend on your specific personality, but there is help, and taking the first steps toward recovery will spur you on to go deeper.

Initial Recovery Exercise

For this exercise, you will want to take your mindfulness to a new level. We've worked on understanding where you hold your tension in your body, but this exercise will help you be more mindful of your stored trauma.

- *Heel Drops*: Begin by standing and allowing your visual focus to soften, so you're not looking at anything in particular. Raise slowly up onto your toes, and then drop back down onto your heels. Do this in a slow rhythm as you imagine that your entire weight is dropping down onto your heels at once. In fact, let it make a loud thud as you do so. Now, bring your attention to your hips and lower back. How does it feel there? Do you feel like the jolt loosened your hips or back? Note the sensations you experience and then try to relax your back and hips. Do this exercise for one minute.

- ***Shaking***: After pausing for a short time after finishing the heel drops, stand again and use your knees to bounce in your legs gently. Keep your knees slightly bent as you push backwards, and then come back to straight again, thereby creating a soft shaking in your legs. Let yourself imagine this shaking rocks through your body, hips, up your torso to your shoulders, and even into your neck. Then, relax your jaw, lower back, and tailbone as if the base of your spine was really heavy. Do this for one minute.

- ***Wave Breathing***: After a short break, stand still and bring your hands to a rest in front of your thighs. Notice your breath. Inhale slowly and reach your chin forward as you glide your hips backward and lean your upper body forward. This will create an arch through your back. Pause for a moment in this position, and then, as you exhale, let your head relax downward as you move your tailbone under your body and forward and around your back. As you do this, gradually come into an upright position. Do these movements for eight breaths. This will help to extend and mobilize your spine, so pay attention to the movement of your spine as well as to how your weight feels through your heels.

- ***Bamboo Swaying***: After another short break, come back to standing and sway gently back and forth, like bamboo in the wind. Do this for a minute and notice how the rocking movement helps you discharge built-up tension. If you feel small tremors in your body, just let them travel through, but try to notice where they're coming from and any other sensations. This is your body releasing tension.

- ***Check In:*** Now, stand still for a moment as you pay attention to the internal sensations you're having. Do you notice a difference in how tense or relaxed you feel? Do you feel a difference in your legs or feet? Do they seem more alive or as if energy is flowing better? Do you feel more connected to the ground than you did before?

Once you've finished these exercises, document everything in your journal. Let yourself write freely as you describe any sensations—emotional or physical—that you experienced while doing this.

Chapter Seven: Leaving the Past Behind—Deep Healing from an Abusive Relationship

Step 7: Going deep to heal from emotional abuse

Now that you have begun the healing process, there are a few techniques you can use to take your healing to a deeper level. Much of what you do—how you act, react, and the thoughts you have—arise out of your childhood experiences. That's why it can be helpful to look at how those experiences might be affecting your choices as an adult. Some people seek out toxic relationships because they have developed core beliefs about what they deserve and what they don't deserve. Some people don't believe they are worthy of happiness because they have a dark side. When we examine these concepts, we can see how they affect most of our choices about our adult relationships. Let's look at two concepts: 1) core beliefs, and 2) your shadow self.

Core Beliefs

Core beliefs are deeply held assumptions we have formed about ourselves, the way the world works, and other people. These are more than simply opinions; they are firmly embedded in our thinking and influence our reality and behavior significantly. In short, nothing matters more than the core beliefs we have formed. They are at the root of our problems and influence how we think. As the name suggests, these are beliefs, not facts, but we act as if they are immutable truths.

You typically form your core beliefs in childhood, and because your child's mind can distort reality, they are very often untrue. Even so, they act like magnets to attract evidence that convinces you they are true, and that makes them stronger. They can, in fact, repel anything that challenges their validity, but it is possible to change them.

Psychologists typically divide core beliefs among three interrelated levels of cognition:

- Core beliefs.
- Dysfunctional assumptions.
- Negative automatic thoughts.

Essentially, negative automatic thoughts are the result of core beliefs and dysfunctional assumptions. Your core beliefs are formed early in your life, and your upbringing plays a critical role in their formation. Given that they form so early in life, they are very deeply embedded in your psyche by the time you reach adulthood. This makes them very difficult to change. At the time you form them, they are acting like coping mechanisms to help you make sense of what you're experiencing. Because you're coming from a place of child-like understanding, these beliefs are commonly distorted, and can, therefore, become unproductive and harmful as you get older.

It is common for harmful core beliefs to be expressed in absolute terms. Examples include sentences that start with, "People are…," "The world is…," or, "I am…" You might come to believe, for example, that you are evil, and you can imagine how that would affect your behavior. Other common core beliefs include thinking one is a loser, not good enough, incompetent, stupid, rotten to the core, boring, flawed, or unlovable. You can also believe that other people are bad, untrustworthy, exploitative, or manipulative. And, finally, you might come to believe that the world itself is a dangerous place. These beliefs can leave you feeling helpless, worthless, and unlovable.

Some people do form positive core beliefs, and these people have no need to change anything, but if you're not among those lucky few, you'll want to change your core beliefs if you want to reach your full potential. The core beliefs you form depend on some of your earliest childhood experiences. Psychologists now realize that you form some basic ideas about the world in the first two years of life. You either come to see the world as a relatively safe place where your needs are met, or you come to see the world as a dangerous place where your needs might not be met. This affects your ability to form attachments to other people. To form healthy relationships, you need to be able to form strong bonds with the people in your life.

If you have come to view the world as an unsafe place; however, that also affects how you think about yourself. You experience less security and don't form healthy attachments. That can leave you extremely vulnerable as you grow into adulthood. But how can you discover your core beliefs? Let's explore a few strategies.

Automatic Negative Thoughts (ANTs)

The negative core beliefs we form at an early age manifest in our present reality as rigid attitudes and rules. For example, if you form a belief that you are not worthy of love, you might implement certain rules like needing to be thin to be lovable. Or, you might think you can never disagree with anyone, lest they determine you are unlovable. Since these negative core beliefs intrude on our present reality in this way, we can use our negative thoughts to look for patterns. You can also look for patterns in your interpretations of your lived experiences to help identify the negative core beliefs you've adopted.

Socratic questioning can also help uncover those same patterns. By delving deeper into the reasons behind why you believe a certain way, you can arrive at the core beliefs guiding those attitudes. A therapist can help with this by asking you to clarify what you mean by certain rigid rules or statements, inquiring about other points of views and the assumptions you make when you say something, or asking for validation of a viewpoint with evidence. These can help to reveal those underlying core beliefs. There are also worksheets that ask you to identify which beliefs they think apply to them. Finally, there are exercises to help you identify and challenge harmful rules and think about alternatives to the ideas you developed.

Understanding Where Your Core Beliefs Came From

Once you've identified your negative core beliefs, the next step is to understand where they originated. When did you first experience thinking about yourself as bad, unlovable, or stupid? What experiences caused you to form those beliefs. Are there people in your family who also feel this way? This can be achieved by using mindfulness techniques to allow yourself to remember the first time you felt that way and explore the circumstances in which the belief first arose.

Challenging the Core Beliefs

After identifying your core beliefs and understanding their origins, it's time to challenge these beliefs. What typically happens in these situations is that the little you who first formed this belief typically did so as a result of cognitive distortions, whereby your young mind couldn't make a more nuanced interpretation of what was happening at the time you formed the core belief. But now you have a more sophisticated, educated brain that can parse the nuances in your beliefs. You can amass evidence that contradicts those core beliefs until finally, you arrive at a point where you can no longer accept them as true and let them go.

For example, let's say your parents' divorced when you were little. It's not uncommon for children to adopt the belief that they were somehow to blame for that, and a typical core belief is that they are bad. That's what their young minds decided caused their parents to fight and finally divorce. If you had adopted this core belief and discovered its origins in your parents' divorce, you can now challenge that belief as an adult who understands that marriages are complicated relationships that involve many factors. Children are rarely to blame for the tension between their parents, and as an adult, you can amass evidence from a great variety of sources to contradict the core belief that you are bad.

Finally, as you go through this process of uncovering and challenging your core beliefs, it's important to have compassion for that little you, so you can understand why she thought the way she did. It's also important to comfort and praise her for your heroic efforts to survive a difficult situation. She got you through it, and for that, she is to be congratulated. Life is tough, and you used coping strategies to survive. If they work, they have accomplished what was necessary. However, they no longer serve you, and it's time to let go of those old strategies and the beliefs they created.

The Dark Side

Your dark side is referred to in psychological circles as your shadow self. It is that part of ourselves of which we're least proud. It's the primitive, selfish impulses that no one wants to admit they have. However, it is also a part of us, and to reject it—to push it further into the shadows—will affect our behavior, including the choices we make as we go through life. You can often recognize some of your shadows by looking at the people you find particularly annoying. What you find annoying about them is typically something you see and don't like about yourself. It is the side of you that you push deep inside yourself and deny that it exists.

Anything you deny in yourself becomes part of your shadow. It is your disowned self, and just like a rejected child, it acts out when it's least convenient to affect your behavior. It never leaves you. It stays with you like the black sheep of your internal family. It is formed when your values are formed in childhood. When you begin to label things as "good" and "bad," you start to reject the parts of yourself you associate with being bad. Perhaps you got angry when you were a child and your parents reprimanded you, so that angry you became a part of your shadow. Maybe you acted silly in class and your teacher shamed you in front of your classmates—now, the silly you is relegated to the dark corners of your psyche.

From that time on, you rejected the parts of you that you associated with being bad, and that created what famed psychologist Carl Jung referred to as the personal shadow. However, Carl Jung also said that, "There is no light without shadow and no psychic wholeness without imperfection." In other words, you must integrate and embrace those shadow parts of yourself to make yourself whole again. By ignoring your shadow self, you will continue to make bad relationship choices, which will impact every one of your existing relationships as well. It will also negatively impact your professional life. So, what should you do?

It Begins with Compassion

The first thing to do when you begin your shadow work is to center yourself by putting yourself in a calm, neutral space. This can be done with meditative self-awareness. Sit quietly and calm your mind. Focus on your breathing and allow yourself to become aware of your body. Once you feel calm, start cultivating self-compassion. Realize the difficulties you've been through and appreciate your amazing survival skills that helped you get through them. Accept yourself with all your flaws. See that insecure you who is accustomed to feeling shame or self-contempt, and instead, give her a hug. Tell her how much you appreciate her resourcefulness for seeing you through some very hard times. Now, as you start to focus on your shadow self, remember that everyone has a shadow, and your goal is not to cast your shadow out, but to embrace that part of yourself.

Next, you must muster your courage and reflect on your behaviors, thoughts, and feelings. Be brutally honest about your shadow behaviors. I am sometimes selfish, greedy, and mean. On occasion, I will engage in those behaviors without a care for anyone else. I can be nasty when I fight, and I can be very judgmental. These are traits I would never want to admit I have. Focus on one shadow self at a time—call out your selfish side, for example. Can you see her there, all small, shameful, insecure, and grasping?

I can see her in myself, but then, I start to treat her like a trusted friend. I ask her why she does those things, and to my amazement, she reveals to me that she wants things for herself and me; things that I tend to give away so I won't be considered selfish. She says we need those things. Suddenly, I can have compassion for her. She's just trying to make sure we have what we need. I can thank her for trying to make sure we get our share. I can embrace and accept her. I tell her I will listen to her input as I make decisions. I assure her I will always be sure we have enough to take care of us. We form a trust and bond, and now I can integrate her into the whole that is me; the whole that includes a selfish side, but that selfish side brings gifts. She's not all bad.

This is true for each of your shadow sides, meaning each ugly trait in yourself that you would reject. For each of those, you need to welcome that part of yourself, understand her motivations, accept her gifts, and embrace her as part of your whole. When you do that, you can truly heal your old wounds and negative core beliefs. You can accept and love yourself with all of your flaws. You can cultivate lasting self-compassion, self-acceptance, and true self-love. Finally, you should record your discoveries in your journal. This work can lead to dissociative behaviors, so it helps to record what you experienced to keep it in your awakened mind. It will also help you process the feelings that will inevitably arise as you go through the process.

Deep Work Exercises

1. Identify your core beliefs

You remember that in an earlier chapter, you carried a notebook with you and recorded your negative thoughts? For that exercise, you came up with positive alternatives. For this exercise, you will identify the patterns you see in those negative thoughts. Can you identify at least three core beliefs reflected in those negative thought patterns? If so, write them down.

Next, try to remember the first time you felt those beliefs. What caused them to form? Can you see how your child's mind distorted the situation to create those beliefs? Can you use your adult mind to challenge them? Can you see the survival strategy you employed as a child to survive the situation? Write down your insights in your journal and let yourself process the feelings that arise through your writing. Once you've worked through your feelings, you will want to substitute the negative core beliefs with positive ones. This retrains your brain to think more positively, which will have numerous long-term benefits. Here are a few examples:

- **Negative belief**: I am not enough.
- **Positive substitute**: I am worthy and deserve good things in my life.

- **Negative belief**: I have to be good to deserve love.
- **Positive substitute**: I deserve love just for being me.

- **Negative belief**: I am helpless.
- **Positive substitute**: I am capable and powerful. I can change my situation.

2. Discover your archetype and her shadows

Jungian psychologists have built upon Carl Jung's work by developing archetypes for both the mature masculine and the mature feminine. Discovering your feminine archetype can help you identify her shadows as well. The four archetypes of the mature feminine include the following with two shadows of each:

- **The Queen**: She is a divine leader responsible for safety and well-being. She must be a wise leader who can guide people toward success while also comforting and helping them navigate unknown territories toward redemption. The Queen must prevail to reap her mostly unconscious benefits, and if she fails in her duties, evil prevails. Her shadow sides are the *weakling*—an ineffectual leader incapable of succeeding—and the *tyrant*—an overly controlling, ruthless leader who will do anything to succeed.

- **The Mother**: She is a caring life-giver who helps to maintain humanity. She is nurturing and loving, but there are shadows. One side is the *careless* *mother* who is distant and neglectful, and thereby, endangers her young. On the other side is the *devouring mother* who destroys her own young with her possessiveness.

- **The Wise Woman**: She is the teacher, the lawyer, and the priest. She is a prophetess, communicator of secret knowledge, healer and mediator, counselor, and spiritual leader. She sees what is unseen, but she has shadows too. They are the *fool* and the *witch*; the fool is hapless, whereas the witch is deliberately abusive.

- **The Lover**: She manifests energy and fertility as found in nature. She is at ease with her deepest and most central values and visions, and she is compassionate and loving. Her shadows are the *frigid woman* who lacks those loving qualities, and the *seductress* who is overly sexualized.

Which of these do you resonate with the most? Write about your insights in your journal, and don't forget to include your shadow sides.

Chapter Eight: What About the Kids? Helping Children Recover from Mental Abuse

Step 8: Healing the family

You might want to stay friendly with your toxic ex for the sake of your children, but the reality is that doing so may not be possible. Make no mistake about it—your children are being affected by your toxic relationship. Even if your partner doesn't specifically target them, which is rare, they see the effects of the toxic behavior on you and your relationship. In the case of the narcissist, the very concept of co-parenting really doesn't exist. So, what can you do to help your children cope?

If your ex is physically abusive, you should definitely take legal steps to get full custody and prevent him from seeing your children again. But, unfortunately, it's more complicated with emotional abuse. It's more difficult to prove, and the children involved don't want to cause problems for their father. They might, just as you might, still love him. In fact, it's likely they do. This is common, even among children who are physically abused. That means you might have to accept that their toxic father will be in their life, and unless you take steps to help them cope, it can leave them with complex PTSD, just like it does you.

One of the best things you can do for your children is to keep a cool head when talking about your ex around them or when interacting with them. They are almost always going to make you angry, that's a given. But you need to stay cool. You're out of the relationship now, and what's important is that your kids need to know that life will remain stable. So, when you have to interact with your ex, here are a few tips:

- **Remain calm with deep breathing**: When you feel your anger rising, step back for a minute or two and take ten deep breaths. Make sure they are the kind that expand your belly, as this will activate your parasympathetic nervous system to help you calm down. It's easy to forget to breathe or strain your breath, and this will only make the situation worse because you're not getting enough oxygen to your brain by doing that.

- **Mindfulness**: By practicing mindfulness techniques to stay present, you can be more aware of both your inner and outer environments. This can help you understand your ex's point of view and exactly the meaning behind what they're trying to say. You want to avoid getting lost in thought about what went wrong in the past or worrying about that will happen in the future; however, instead, focus on each moment and stop yourself from becoming too lost in your anger.

When you can control yourself, there are some other steps you can take to help the children and ensure they will feel loved and secure. Let's look at a few of these.

1. **Minimize your contact with your ex**: Your toxic ex will want to continue to engage you in a psychological battle. They use this tactic so they can keep you engaged in the relationship, and that will stay true, even years following your divorce or separation. They will also likely expose your child to the same toxic behavior and mental warfare. Minimizing contact for yourself and your child is your best option if you can't keep him from seeing them altogether. Selfishness is a common characteristic of toxic people, so one strategy you can use to counter it is to make it difficult for them to see your child. Move far away so he has to travel to see them. Do what you can to minimize contact.

2. **Co-parenting plan**: One of the best strategies you can develop is a co-parenting plan that is put in writing. This will define everyone's roles and set boundaries, like visiting or calling times among other scheduling items. If the plan wasn't included as part of the custody agreement, you'll want to legalize it with an

attorney. An attorney can help keep your narcissistic partner in check. It's also best if you use a neutral mediator to help you and your ex draft it.

3. **Guardian Ad Litem (GAL)**: It worthwhile to consider taking advantage of the court system. You can have a guardian ad litem (GAL) appointed for your child. A GAL is a neutral person who is appointed to look out for the best interests of the child. You can request one if you expect that arriving at an agreement with your ex will be too difficult. The GAL becomes familiar with your child and their individual situation, and they make recommendations to the court regarding the best way to divide up custody. They might, for example, help determine where your child will spend the majority of their time or how much contact the child should have with you both.

A mediator, on the other hand, is more of a go-between to help facilitate communication and arrive at a resolution for any disputes. In some cases, a mediator might be required for custody disputes, whereas in other situations, their assistance would be optional. They can help you and your ex resolve issues brought to the court. They won't give advice or orders, but they can help you both work through your parenting plan fairly. Once you have finished the plan, it will be brought to a judge. After approval, the judge will order the plan to be followed as part of the custody arrangement.

4. **Firm boundaries**: Firm boundaries can provide your children with safe, predictable, and secure buffers against the insidious psychological damage done by a toxic parent. A narcissistic parent, for example, creates an emotional roller coaster for their children, which can be even more damaging than physical abuse. It's definitely more insidious. By giving your child a structured environment, you can help offset the damage done by your emotionally unpredictable ex.

5. **Don't feel sorry for your child**: If you pity your child, you will perpetuate a victim mentality, and that will prevent them from moving forward in life. They will also have more trouble learning to create healthy relationships. They don't deserve the toxic

treatment, but feeling sorry for them also won't help.

6. **Be calm, non-emotional, and pleasant in your interactions with your ex**: This might be difficult—even Herculean—but you must do this for the sake of your child. They need to know that they have one parent who can be trusted to act in a consistent and rational manner. By getting pulled into your ex's emotional intensity, you undermine that image for your children.

7. **Limit telephone/texting between your ex and your child while they are in your custody, and vice versa**: The best scenario to employ is no contact at all between him and your child when the child is with you and between you and your child when the child is with him. Stay out of your ex's house so you don't trigger toxic behavior in your ex toward your child. When the child is with you, limiting contact from your ex will help them feel safe and secure in your home. The one upside to staying out of the relationship between your ex and your child is that it will teach your child some valuable coping skills for dealing with toxic people in the future. This is particularly true if you can help them learn healthy coping skills as they go along.

8. **Teach/model social and emotional intelligence**: Help your child develop good social and emotional skills as much as you can. Point out positive traits and teach them about proper emotional regulation and healthy coping skills. Let them see what you do to heal yourself. Keep the lines of communication open at all times, particularly when there is an extreme narcissist in their life. This will help you understand any problems they may be having, and that will help you teach them coping skills they can use to deal with the toxic behavior.

9. **Nurture your child's uniqueness and foster their independence**: If your toxic ex ever had focus on their child, they often lose that between the child's infancy and their adolescent years. They stop seeing the children as a distinct individual with feelings and needs that should be validated and met. In effect, they see the child as an extension of themselves. They interpret normal emotional growth as selfish or deficient, and they mirror that to the child. The child has to meet the needs of the toxic parent—whether those needs are clear or not—to get their approval. To counteract the effects of this, be sure you're appreciating their uniqueness as an individual and encouraging them to develop their independence.

10. **Don't criticize your ex in front of your child**: This is never a good thing to do, no matter the circumstances; no matter how mature you might think your child is and no matter how bad your toxic ex's behavior is, your child is not equipped to deal with this. It's often complicated by how your toxic ex can project normal behavior to the rest of society, so your criticism can seem out of step. Help your child deal with your ex's toxic behavior, but do so without criticizing him. Your child might come to resent you if you don't.

11. **Don't think of yourself as a partner with your ex when it comes to your child**: It's admirable to want to work things out for the sake of your child, but it simply can't work with a narcissistic partner. You must take steps to heal yourself and help your child heal as much as you can, but that will not be achieved by trying to partner with your ex as you parent your child. Instead, focus on establishing a warm, nurturing, and safe home where your child can grow and develop into a healthy adult.

Of course, if your child has major difficulties, such as struggling with depression, suicidal thoughts, severe anxiety, acting out in school or at home, it's best to seek professional help, and the sooner the better. They will need guidance from you, but sometimes it takes an objective third party to help them express their feelings. In fact, it can be helpful in any case to take them to a therapist following the breakup. They will use a variety of techniques to help your child develop healthy coping strategies.

Exercises for Helping Your Child Heal

It's vital to keep the lines of communication open with your child, but they are dealing with some complex emotions and may not know how to express themselves. These exercises can help you teach them healthy ways to express what they're feeling.

1. **Drawing with younger children**: Your younger children will have a myriad of emotions about your separation or divorce. These include worry, sadness, relief, guilt, embarrassment, loneliness, and anxiety, among others. Younger children, in particular, can have problems expressing what they're feeling. However, they can often draw pictures to express their emotions rather than words. You can prompt them with the following questions and instructions:
   a. Can you draw what divorce looks like?

b. Can you draw a picture of how you feel now that your daddy and I are divorced?

c. Draw a picture of anger, sadness, or loneliness.

d. Draw a picture of your family. Include everyone you consider to be a part of your family and write their names by their picture.

e. Draw a picture of the homes where you live.

f. If a genie would grant you one wish for your family, what would you wish for? Draw a picture of it.

Once your child has drawn their picture, encourage them to talk about it. Ask them questions about what they have drawn and provide positive support for their answers and efforts to communicate.

2. **Starting a conversation with older children**: Children who are old enough to understand better what is happening can still have problems expressing their fears, worries, and questions about the divorce. If you can help them feel comfortable talking to you about their feelings, it can help ease their adjustment to the new reality. One way to do this is to have a conversation with them. This can happen during dinner, in the car, at bedtime, on walks, or in any other setting where they

will feel comfortable opening up to you. You can help open them up with the following questions:

    a. How has your life changed since the divorce?

    b. Why do you think we got divorced?

    c. Why do you think we got married in the first place?

    d. How do you define a happy family?

    e. Who do you talk to about the divorce?

    f. What are some good things that have happened because of the divorce?

    g. What are you worried about?

    h. What do you think life will be like in five years?

    i. What are some good qualities that your father has?

    j. What are some good qualities that I have?

    k. If you could change anything about your life, what would it be?

Listen patiently to their answers and don't judge what they say. Provide positive support as they express their feelings, so they will feel comfortable talking to you about it again. When you are alone, be sure to write in your journal about the feelings that came up for you while you were helping your child express themselves.

Chapter Nine: How Do I Make a New Life? Reinventing Your Psychopath-Free Life

Step 9: Renewal

Now that you've worked through several different healing exercises, it's time to discuss how you can go about reimagining your life without your toxic ex. Once you have dealt with your fears about being on your own, you will realize that the world is, indeed, your oyster. You can pursue your goals without having to worry about how your partner feels about it. It's your time to determine what's important to you and start working toward what you want to achieve for your life. As you dream your future into existence, the sky's the limit.

The Wheel of Life

Begin by using the Wheel of Life—see the figure below—to rate each area of your life on a scale of 1-10. Rate each area in accordance with how you feel right now. This will help you to determine the weakest and strongest points of your life. Once you know that, you can figure out what areas need improvement and which are doing pretty well. You can celebrate the good areas, and once you know your weak ones, you can place your focus on them. You would do that by dreaming.

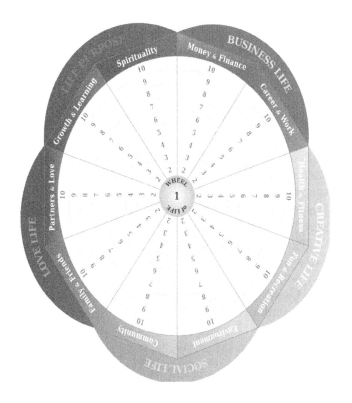

Dream!

You can begin this process by determining what you want in life, and you can do this for each area of your life. What do you want for your professional life? What do you want for your personal life moving forward? What about your hobbies? For each area of your life, you will want to determine your goals and how you will go about reaching them. You can start with a simple exercise: complete the following sentence 15 times: "My life is ideal when…" The words you use to finish the sentence should be verbs. For example, "My life is ideal when I'm helping people achieve a healthy level of fitness," or, "My life is ideal when I'm expressing my creativity through my writing."

Once you've finished completing the sentence 15 times, choose the five most important sentences and find patterns. Do you believe your life is ideal when you're helping someone else in some way? Do you believe it's ideal when you're doing something creative? Maybe you believe it's ideal when you are achieving financial independence and not having to work anymore. Whatever patterns you see, write these down as values for your life. For example, one value when you're helping people is to be of service to others. Another value might be creative expression or complete independence.

Next, take a look at the types of activities you listed for your ideal life and make a list of how you might achieve those goals. For example, if you listed helping people to achieve their fitness goals, you could achieve that by becoming a personal trainer. You could also achieve that by becoming a physical therapist or a dietician. Once you have a list of the varied ways you could achieve your ideal life, determine what resonates the most with you. Maybe you would like to combine helping people as a personal trainer with being able to work independently. Once you've identified a specific goal to pursue, you can then determine what you need to do to achieve your ideal life.

Setting Goals

Now that you've identified what would make every aspect of your life ideal, you can set goals to achieve your dream life. For each one of your goals, make a list of what would be needed to achieve it. For example, if you wanted to become a personal trainer, do you need to get certified? If you need to get certified, what will that entail? Do you need specific training? If you need specific training, how do you get that? Do you need to enroll in a school or find someone to train you? If you need to do that, how much money and time do you need to do it? Each of these stepping stones to achieving your ultimate goal would now become milestones that will get you closer to your ideal life.

After you have identified your milestones, you can determine a timeline for achieving each milestone and the main stages toward achieving your ultimate goal. For example, let's say you determine you will need to be trained by a professional trainer, after which you will need to pass a test to become certified yourself. Then, you will need to develop a business plan for attracting clients and getting enough to support yourself with only your personal training business. Maybe you would also like to have a gym where you can train your clients. You can set up your milestones into groups. Group 1 would relate to getting your certificate, Group 2 would relate to setting up your business, and Group 3 would relate to attracting clients.

From there, you can estimate the time and money you need for each stage, and then you can begin working on achieving those milestones. It's also important to celebrate even the minor milestones, so you can stay motivated to keep going. It can help toward this end to make a vision board and place it somewhere you'll see everyday. This board would have images and motivational sayings to help you remember why you're doing this.

Planning Meetings

In your new life, you're now your own project manager, so act like it. Plan meetings with yourself to decide your day, week, month, and year. For each day, determine what steps you will take that day to work toward your next milestone. Each week, make note of your achievements, pat yourself on the back by taking yourself out to dinner or doing something you love to do, and plan for the next week. At your monthly meetings, you can take note of your progress and whether it's sufficient for achieving your yearly goals. If it's moving too slowly or you run into obstacles, you can make adjustments as necessary. Finally, at the yearly planning meeting, you can review your progress and make adjustments, if that is required. You can also plan for the next year.

These planning meetings will help you stay motivated, chart your progress, and stay on track with your goals. It might seem like what you want for your life will take forever to achieve, but once you're making progress, you'll be surprised at how quickly you're getting closer to your goals. Remember that the time between right now and when you are living your ideal life will pass no matter what, so you may as well be making progress toward your dreams.

Tips for Enjoying the Ride

It's also important to enjoy yourself while you're reaching for that brass ring. Toward that end, you might want to incorporate the following tips to help you have a little fun along the way.

- **Incorporate daily meditation into your routine**: This will help you stay calm and clarify your goals. You'll also gain valuable insights into your dream life.

- **Stay healthy**: It's vital to stay physically healthy so you can have the energy to do what you have to do. Toward that end, you'll want to exercise daily to stay fit, and it also causes your brain to release endorphins—those feel-good chemicals that boost your mood. Eating healthy is another factor here. Be sure you're treating your body right so it can do what you need it to do to help you achieve your ideal life.

- **Play**: One of the best things you can do for yourself is play like you did when you were a kid and didn't have a care in the world. It's great for your mental health, energy, and motivation. Make time each day for something you enjoy doing, and plan each week for the things that take more time.

- **Surround yourself with positive people**: We've mentioned this before, but it's worth mentioning again. These people have your best interests at heart and be willing to provide you with positive, uplifting, and motivational feedback to help you achieve your dreams. Get rid of anyone who doesn't do that for you. You've had one toxic relationship; you don't need any more!

•

Reinvention Exercise

You'll want to practice this exercise at least once a day. It's best to do it right after waking in the morning so you set the tone for the day, and again, before going to sleep at night. It will set your brain to working unconsciously to help your dreams come true. To begin, center yourself with mindfulness meditation and start reimagining your life. Visualize your ideal life, in whatever way you would define that. However, you need to do more than simply visualize it; really let yourself *feel* it. Imagine you have achieved all your goals. What will your life feel like? What will it look like? What will it smell like? How will it affect your actions? Really let yourself live in that moment as if it is already true. Are you excited or joyful? Can you feel the fine clothing you wear on your skin? Can you bask in the positive reviews of your artwork? By engaging all your senses in this exercise, you will train your brain to look for ways to achieve your dreams.

Chapter Ten: New Beginnings— Preparing For and Building Healthy New Relationships

Step 10: Live and learn from your toxic relationship

Now that you've been healing from your toxic relationship and rebuilding your life, it's time to get back on the horse you fell off of. It's time to prepare for and build healthier relationships. You will reimagine your intimate, romantic partnerships going forward. The first step in this process is understanding what a healthy relationship looks like.

Healthy Relationships

You've already been exposed to a toxic relationship, but you might not have ever experienced a healthy one. Perhaps you did, but it was so long ago that you've forgotten what it felt like. It's time to remind yourself as you plan to move on with that part of your life. The following characteristics are all non-negotiable for creating a healthy relationship. If any one of them is missing, it's a problem you'll need to address.

- **Trust**: This is probably the single most important characteristic of a healthy relationship. It's the foundation upon which you can build emotional intimacy. It refers not only to faithfulness, but also to the idea that you can trust your partner to come through for you, you can believe what they're saying, and you can trust them to work with you to resolve problems. Without trust, your relationship is extremely vulnerable to stress and uncertainty.

- **Communication**: This is not something that comes easily to everyone, but it's vital to a healthy relationship. You have to work on keeping the lines of communication open and creating a safe environment for each partner to express themselves freely. Don't judge what your partner says; accept their point of view with loving understanding and be honest and open in your expression of your needs and desires. That's the only way for your relationship to remain strong and grow.

- **Patience**: Everyone makes mistakes from time to time, so be patient and compassionate with your partner. By being patient, you offer your partner peace, flexibility, and support, even when they're having a bad day. They'll return the favor when it's your turn to have an off day. Being patient allows you both to feel unconditionally loved.

- **Empathy**: Perhaps one of the best ways to understand your partner is to put yourself in their shoes. When you put forth the effort to understand their perspective truly, it fosters a compassionate perspective for understanding their essential humanity. It's a crucial characteristic for long-term love.

- **Affection and interest**: Everyone needs to feel loved and desired by their intimate partner. It's what makes you a couple, so don't stop letting them know you care. Hug them, touch them affectionately, kiss them passionately, and tell them you love them often. Show them you're interested in them at the deepest, most intimate level.

- **Flexibility**: If you want your relationship to last, you must learn to compromise. This doesn't mean compromising your values, but it does mean working with your partner to resolve problems that arise. You're sharing a life together, and that requires compromise to make it work.

- **Appreciation**: Show your gratitude for all the things your partner does for you. You need to say and show it with affectionate gestures. The more you show your partner you appreciate them, the more they will want to do things for you, and the more you'll want to return the favor. This is how you nourish a healthy relationship.

- **Room for Growth:** Over time, both you and your partner will change. Your relationship has to allow for both personal and shared growth. Without it, you'll feel stuck, and that will drive you apart. Work on growing together so your relationship can survive the changes it will inevitably go through.

- **Respect**: Respect is essential in your intimate relationships. You should never want to debase or belittle someone you love. You should want to validate their emotions and dreams. You should value their opinion, protect each other's privacy, and treasure the time you spend with them. If you lose respect for your partner, the relationship will soon be lost.

- **Reciprocity**: Relationships are always full of give and take; he does something for you and you return the favor. He picks up the slack when you're having a difficult time, and you do the same for him when he's down. It won't always work out exactly and equally, but both partners need to believe their efforts will be returned in some way for the relationship to last.

- **Healthy Conflict Resolution**: The way a couple argues can predict the fate of their relationship. You've already experienced a toxic relationship. Going forward, be certain you and your partner practice healthy ways to resolve conflicts. Remember that this is someone you love deeply. When there are disagreements, respect their point of view and work to resolve the problem to the satisfaction of everyone concerned.

- **Individuality and Boundaries**: You must retain your sense of self in order to create a healthy relationship. You need to have your own space and time to do things that define you as an individual. Set boundaries to ensure you get what you need to maintain your individuality, even as you work together toward your shared goals.

- **Openness and Honesty**: This is equally critical to develop a lasting relationship. You must be able to tell your partner what you need, like, and don't like. You need to feel like you can tell them and they will respect your needs, opinions, and desires. A relationship full of deceit simply cannot last.

These are the characteristics that indicate a healthy relationship. There may be more, but without these traits to build a strong foundation, your relationship won't be healthy, and it likely won't last.

Starting Anew

It's one thing to know what is required for a healthy relationship, but it's not uncommon for women who have suffered emotional abuse to have real fear about starting over again. This is particularly true if, like me, you thought you were getting into a healthy relationship when it started. There are a few ways you can get back into the dating world in a way that will make you feel more secure. The key is to take it slow. Don't jump into a new relationship too fast.

You might try telling yourself that you're just practicing for a new, healthy relationship. As you get back into the dating pool, it's important to choose good men who respect and treat you well. When you go on dates, listen to your heart and gut. Be open with your emotions, but if anything feels off to you—if you notice any strange behavior or he suddenly makes you feel guilty at all—it's time to run away. That is not the man for you.

You want your romantic partner to be your friend too. Many stable, healthy relationships are based on mutual friendship and respect, so take it slowly and let the friendship grow before it blooms into romance. Remember that your previous, toxic relationship developed at light speed, and it was full of a wide range of emotions, a veritable roller coaster ride. You don't want or need another codependent relationship; you need and deserve to live your life enjoying every moment and having it full of love. By taking it slowly and respecting yourself, I have no doubt that new love will happen to you soon!

What About Me?

Before my divorce, I went to the seaside for a little relaxation. I wanted to have enough energy for what was coming up, and I also wanted a sexy suntan on my face. I wore all black for my divorce and got nothing—just a whole me again, and I was free. My ex didn't say a word to me, like I was nothing. I thanked him for our relationships and wished him good luck in his life. In the days following my divorce, I met a regular guy on Tinder. He invited me for lunch, and I thought, "Why not?" I didn't think he was my type, but I decided to go just to have someone to chat with. Our first date was just so-so. It was boring, and he was dull as well. He wasn't very sexy, strong, tall, or masculine. What's more, I felt pity for him because he was also freshly divorced. After that first lunch, I was looking for a reason to run away. But, time passed, and we kept chatting about our experiences with relationships. In fact, we became good friends after a month or so. We went to the movies and cafes together. After about a year, we fell in love and began dating as a couple. This has become the most healthy, adult relationship I have ever had. I don't know if we will be together forever, or even how long we might be together; however, I do know that we respect one another, take care of our relationship, and cherish it as something that's precious and fragile. Love will come, just keep your heart open!

New Beginnings Exercises

Exercise #1: Identify your ideal relationship: Begin by writing down what you want to have in what you see as your ideal romantic relationship. What are the five most important things you want in a romantic partner? What are five things you absolutely won't tolerate? What do you feel for your ideal partner? How are the two of you together? How does he make you feel about yourself?

Exercise #2: Describe him: In your journal, describe every detail about your perfect partner. Be sure to include everything about him—his looks, age, job, character, income—everything. What does he like to do? What are his interests and hobbies? What are the things about him that you might not like but are willing to tolerate? What kinds of things would you not put up with?

Some women might be attracted to a strong, masculine, handsome man, but some men like that can be rude, and any man can be toxic. Narcissists are a good example. You also have to consider carefully what you consider masculine. Some women are accustomed to abuse, and they come to see that as attractive. This is particularly true if they have been abused in childhood. If their father was abusive, that's their model for manliness, and this tends to be what they look for as an adult. But remember that you're trying to break those old habits, so consider carefully if you want to keep repeating the same experiences.

Exercise #3: Once a little time has passed and you have had the opportunity to learn about healthy relationships, it's time to consider what mistakes you made in your past relationship. What did you allow that you now know you would never do again? How can you set better boundaries? What would happen if someone seemed nice but started treating you badly? In what way did you act inappropriately? How will you avoid your past mistakes?

Final Exercise: Take the Pledge

Now that you've lived through and freed yourself from a toxic relationship, healed your complex PTSD after freeing yourself, and learned what a healthy relationship looks like, it's time to take the pledge to never allow yourself to become involved with a toxic psychopath again. Toward that end, raise your right hand and repeat the following pledge out loud:

Your Pledge for Your New Life

1. I deserve to be loved, and I know now what love looks like, so I will not accept anything less from a romantic partner.

2. I will trust my gut instinct. If it doesn't feel right, I won't ignore that. I won't make excuses. I will trust myself and face the problem head-on.

3. I deserve to be respected, and if I see that I am not being respected, I will not tolerate that kind of treatment.

4. I will ask myself the question: "Would I treat my partner like this?" If the answer is no, then I know I don't deserve that treatment either.

5. Anyone who would make me beg for their love or attention is not worth the love I have to share with them. I will never again beg for someone to be or stay in my life.

6. I will not tolerate being criticized about my physical appearance or other parts of my life, including my body, weight, job, age, or any other insecurity I might choose to share with an intimate partner. A truly loving and good partner would never put me down. They would want to lift me up.

7. My relationships will all be equal and mutual. I understand that love is not about control and power.

8. Each month, I will step back and determine whether I am being truly loved and respected, not flattered or love-bombed.

9. I will not put up with someone who speaks to me sarcastically or condescendingly. A loving partner will not patronize me.

10. I will choose to be single rather than in a toxic relationship.

11. I will not tolerate projection. I will not permit my partner to call me jealous, crazy, or any other characteristic that he might project onto me that is true of him.

12. If I am ever uncertain about these points, I will seek out help from a good friend, support group, or therapist. I will not act or react impulsively. However, I will act if I determine my partner is not living up to the tenets of this pledge.

Now, write this pledge in your journal and sign your name. You're affirming your love and respect for yourself by doing so.

Final Words

Congratulations on deciding to take action to reclaim your life! The steps in this book will help you recover from your experience in a toxic relationship and reclaim the happy life you have a right to live. You deserve to have happiness in your life. You deserve to be treated with respect. You deserve a truly healthy and loving relationship.

Unfortunately, not everyone is capable of giving that to you. Your former partner may have had a difficult life that left him with scars he has yet to overcome. That's a tragedy, but you shouldn't be made to suffer for the trauma he suffered at the hands of others. You have a right to live a happy life—one that includes self-respect, self-love, and a healthy relationship with a loving partner.

You can't heal your partner, but you can heal yourself. You've taken the steps to do that. Now that you're well on your way to recovery, don't give up. Keep putting into practice the healthy activities we've described in this book. Your life is out there waiting for you, and you deserve for it to be the life of your dreams. Don't ever settle for less. You are a survivor, not a victim, and as such, you can achieve any goal you set for yourself. You can have it all, and you deserve it. I believe in you. You are a phoenix rising from the ashes of a living hell, and you will go on to shine as bright as the sun!

It is my sincere desire that this book has helped you heal your trauma. I would truly love to hear your feedback and learn how you've gone on to live your dreams. Please take a moment to leave your review on Amazon, so I can hear your story. It's also helpful for other readers to determine if this book might help them as well. It helps new authors like myself get their work out there. Your support is crucial, and I appreciate your feedback. I hope to be hearing about your success soon!

Thank you!

Be brave and become the best version of yourself. Reclaim your life and live your dreams!

Warm regards,

Elena Miro.

Discover my Other Book